USE OF COPYRIGHTED MUSIC

A licence issued by Concord Theatricals to perform this play does
not include permission to use the incidental music specified in this
publication. In the United Kingdom: Where the place of performance
is already licensed by the PERFORMING RIGHT SOCIETY (PRS)
a return of the music used must be made to them. If the place of
performance is not so licensed then application should be made to PRS
for Music (www.prsformusic.com). A separate and additional licence
from PHONOGRAPHIC PERFORMANCE LTD (www.ppluk.com) may
be needed whenever commercial recordings are used. Outside the United
Kingdom: Please contact the appropriate music licensing authority in
your territory for the rights to any incidental music.

USE OF COPYRIGHTED THIRD-PARTY MATERIALS

Licensees are solely responsible for obtaining formal written permission
from copyright owners to use copyrighted third-party materials (e.g.,
artworks, logos) in the performance of this play and are strongly cautioned
to do so. If no such permission is obtained by the licensee, then the
licensee must use only original materials that the licensee owns and
controls. Licensees are solely responsible and liable for clearances of all
third-party copyrighted materials, and shall indemnify the copyright
owners of the play(s) and their licensing agent, Concord Theatricals Ltd.,
against any costs, expenses, losses and liabilities arising from the use of
such copyrighted third-party materials by licensees.

IMPORTANT BILLING AND CREDIT REQUIREMENTS

If you have obtained performance rights to this title, please refer to your
licensing agreement for important billing and credit requirements.

NOTE

This edition reflects a rehearsal draft of the script and may differ from the
final production.

A WOMAN WALKS INTO A BANK was first produced by and performed at Theatre503 (Artistic Director, Lisa Spirling; Executive Director, Emily Carewe), London, on 21st November 2023. The cast was as follows:

A / AN OLD WOMAN ....Giulia Innocenti
B / A YOUNG MAN.................................Sam Newton
C / A DEBT COLLECTOR ....Keith Dunphy

The creative team and production team were as follows:

WRITER AND DIRECTOR ....Roxy Cook
SET AND COSTUME DESIGNER........................David Allen
LIGHTING DESIGNER.................................. Joe Price
SOUND DESIGNER AND COMPOSER .... Hugh Sheehan
ASSOCIATE DIRECTOR
AND MOVEMENT DIRECTOR......................... Sam Hooper
CASTING DIRECTOR........................ Nadine Rennie CDG
ASSOCIATE LIGHTING DESIGNER................Nicola Crawford
PRODUCTION MANAGER............................ Misha Mah
STAGE MANAGER ....Rose Hockaday
ASSISTANT STAGE MANAGER
ON PLACEMENT .... Amie Whickman
PRODUCER .... Ceri Lothian
ASSISTANT PRODUCER........................Humnah Abdullah
PR .... Nicole Poole PR

A WOMAN WALKS INTO A BANK

by Roxy Cook

ılı SAMUEL FRENCH ılı

FOR AMATEUR PRODUCTION ENQUIRIES

UNITED KINGDOM AND WORLD
EXCLUDING NORTH AMERICA
licensing@concordtheatricals.co.uk
020-7054-7298

Each title is subject to availability from Concord Theatricals,
depending upon country of performance.

CHARACTERS

This play is narrated by three storytellers: **A**, **B** and **C**, each with their own distinct personalities and opinions. As the piece progresses, they take on more and more responsibility for one of three main characters...

A – plays an old woman (82 years)

B – plays a young man (25 years)

C – plays a debt collector (59 years)

A, B and **C** also all play a cat called Sally (18 years)

SETTING

Moscow, Russia.

TIME

Act One: One day in July 2018, shortly after the World Cup.

Act Two: 6th January 2019, Russian Orthodox Christmas Eve.

AUTHOR'S NOTES

No Russian accents

/ = an interruption

ABOUT THEATRE503

Theatre503 is at the forefront of identifying and nurturing new voices at the very start of their careers and launching them into the industry. They stage more early-career playwrights than any other theatre in the world – with over one hundred and twenty writers premiered each year from festivals of short pieces to full length productions, resulting in employment for over one thousand freelance artists through their year-round programme.

Theatre503 provides a diverse pipeline of talent resulting in modern classics like *The Mountaintop* by Katori Hall and *Rotterdam* by Jon Brittain – both Olivier Award winners – to future classics like Yasmin Joseph's *J'Ouvert*, winner of the 2020 James Tait Black Prize and transferred to the West End/BBC Arts and *Wolfie* by Ross Willis, winner of the 2020 Writers Guild Award for Best New Play. Writers who began their creative life at Theatre503 are now writing for the likes of *The Crown, Succession, Doctor Who, Killing Eve* and *Normal People* and every single major subsidised theatre in the country now boasts a new play by a writer who started at Theatre503.

THEATRE503 TEAM

Artistic Director	Lisa Spirling
Executive Director	Emily Carewe
Literary Manager	Steve Harper
Producer	Ceri Lothian
General Manager	Emily Dickson
Carne Associate Director	Kalungi Ssebandeke
Literary Associate	Lauretta Barrow
Assistant Producer	Humnah Abdullah
Technical Manager	Misha Mah
Marketing Officer	Millie Whittam
Administrator	Lizzie Akita
Development Coordinator	Heloise Gillingham

THEATRE503 BOARD

Erica Whyman OBE (Chair)
Royce Bell (Co-Vice Chair)
Emma Rees (Co-Vice Chair)
Eleanor Lloyd
Jack Tilbury
Ollie Raggett
Roy Williams OBE
Zena Tuitt
Joshua Chua

Theatre503 would like to thank Philip and Christine Carne, sponsors of the Carne Prize, and Samuel French Ltd for their generous support of the Theatre503 International Playwriting Award.

Thanks to all the 2023 Theatre503 International Playwriting Award Readers: Almiro Andrade, Tian Brown-Sampson, Lisa Cagnacci, Lou Corben, Sujana Crawford, Amy Bethan Evans, Adam Goodall, William Gregory, Neil Grutchfield, Isabelle Kassam, Erick Kwashie, Tom Latter, Kyle Marsh, Robbie Nestor, Nika Obydzinski, Gugulethu Oka Mseleku, Shefali Parmar, Fatima Serghini, Andrew Skipper, Audrey Thayer, Pravin Wilkins, Beth Wilson.

Additional thanks to Ann Joseph and Corinne Rooney for OCourant, Celia Dugua, Clemence Reubourg, Double Slice Studio, Frank Herfort Photography, Shaz McGee, Pushkin House, and Theatre Deli.

This production has been supported by The Christina Smith Foundation, The Golsoncott Foundation, The Royal Victoria Hall Foundation and The Unity Theatre Trust.

Theatre503's work would not be possible without the support of the following individuals, trusts and organisations:

We are particularly grateful to Philip and Christine Carne and the long-term support of The Carne Trust for our International Playwriting Award, the 503 Five and Carne Associate.

503Patrons: Ayla & Jon Hill, Berlin Associates, Caroline & Tim Langton, Cas & Philip Donald, Catharine Roos, Céline Gagnon, David Baxter & Carol Rahn, DavidsonMorris Solicitors, Eilene Davidson, Eric Bensaude, Erica Whyman, Freddie Hutchins & Oliver Rawlins, Gaskell & Jennifer Jacobs, Geraldine Sharpe-Newton, Ian Mill KC, Jack Tilbury/Plann, Laura Riddeck, Lisa Swinney, Lou Wilks & Tom Gowans, Louise Rawlins, Marcus Markou, Marianne Badrichani, Matthew Marren, Nick Hern Books, Pam Alexander & Roger Booker, Robert O'Dowd, Sally O'Neill, Sean Winnett, Steve Winter, The Bell Family, The Bloor Family, United Agents and all our 503Friends and Share the Drama supporters.

503 Slate Philanthropic Co-Producers: Cas & Philip Donald, Concord Music Group, Inc, Eilene Davidson, Gordon Bloor, Hania Farrell, Jean Doumanian/Peony NY LLC, Kater Gordon Productions Ltd, Kofi Owusu Bempah, Lucas Achkar, Marcus Markou, Ocourant Ltd, Royce Bell, Trish Wadley Productions.

Arts Council England Grants for the Arts, Backstage Trust, Battersea Power Station Foundation (Right to Write), Cockayne Grants for the Arts (503 Productions), Concord Theatricals (503 Playwriting Award), Garrick Charitable Trust, Gregory Annenberg Weingarten, GRoW @ Annenberg, Noel Coward Foundation (Rapid Write Response), Theatres Trust, The de Laszlo Foundation, The Foyle Foundation, The Orseis Trust (503Five), Wandsworth Borough Council, Wimbledon Foundation (Five-O-Fresh).

Our ongoing thanks and gratitude to Three Cheers Pub Co. for our home above The Latchmere Pub.

CAST

A / AN OLD WOMAN | Giulia Innocenti

This is Giulia's first time at Theatre503. She recently played "Nelly" in Inspector Sands' UK tour of *Wuthering Heights*. Giulia is a founding member and Co-Artistic Director of Inspector Sands and has devised and performed in all their shows to date, including *Hysteria*, *If That's All There Is*, *Rock Pool*, *Mass Observation*, and *The Lounge*.

Other theatre credits include: *The Elephantom* (National Theatre); *Cinderella* (Oxford Playhouse); *The Merry Wives of Windsor*, *The Mouse and His Child*, *The 13 Midnight Challenges of Angelus Diablo* (RSC); *Cymbeline* (Kneehigh); *Sisters...* (The Gate); *One Thousand Paper Cranes* (Catherine Wheel); *The Grimm Tales*, *The Nutcracker and the Mouse King* (Unicorn Theatre); *Madam Butterfly* (ENO); *Low Life*, *1984* (Blind Summit); *Lady Macbeth's Factory* (Quebracho Theatre); *Peer Gynt* (Arcola); *Wagner's Dream* (The Barbican); *Prince Charming* (Little Angel).

Feature Film: *Near Miss* (Bandit Country); *Heart of Stone* (Netflix). **Radio:** *The Continuity Man* (BBC).

B / A YOUNG MAN | Sam Newton

Sam is an actor and mover from Birmingham.

Stage credits include: *The Curious Incident of the Dog in the Night-Time* (West End & UK/International Tour); *Big Big Sky* by Tom Wells (Hampstead Theatre); Frantic Assembly's *Sometimes Thinking* (River Stage); and Nigel Slater's *Toast* (The Lowry/Traverse).

Screen credits include: *Newark, Newark* (UKTV Gold), *The Bastard Son and The Devil Himself* (Netflix) & *Casualty* (BBC).

C / A DEBT COLLECTOR | Keith Dunphy

Keith recently filmed *The Winter King* (Sony/Badwolf Productions). He also is devising and performing *This Modern Colossus*, a solo theatre show, to be performed Autumn 2023/2024. Keith has previously trained at RADA.

Stage credits include: *Under The Black Rock* (Arcola Theatre); *Fighting Irish* (Belgrade Theatre); *The Lovely Bones* (UK Tour); *Easter Rising and There After* (Jermyn St Theatre); *The Rivals* (Bristol Old Vic); *The Birthday Party* (Royal Exchange Theatre); *One For The Road, Victoria Station* (Young Vic Theatre and the Print Rooms); *Macbeth* (The Globe Theatre); *Romeo and Juliet, The Grapes of Wrath, Catastrophic Sex Music* (Mercury Theatre); *Histories Company* (Royal Shakespeare Company); *Lime Tree Bower* (Theatre503)

Screen credits include: *The Winter King*; *Rebellion*; *No Offence*; *Beowulf*; *The Hollow Crown*; *Peaky Blinders*; *Life Begins*; *Ultimate Force*; *Professor T*; *The Banishing*; *Rogue One*; *The Spoiler*; *Les Misérables*; *Black Death*; *Children of Men*; *The Wind That Shakes the Barley*; *Inside I'm Dancing*.

CREATIVES

Writer and Director | Roxy Cook
Roxy is a writer, director and dramaturg working across theatre and TV. After graduating from Mountview, she spent five years directing new writing. Roxy began writing in 2019 and *A Woman Walks Into a Bank* is her first play. It was shortlisted for the Women's Prize for Playwriting 2021 and longlisted for the Bruntwood Prize and Verity Bargate Award, both 2022. Outside of theatre, Roxy works in development and script editing for TV.
Theatre highlights: Director of *Happy to Help* (Park Theatre); associate director of Jon Brittain's Olivier Award winning *Rotterdam* (Theatre503, Trafalgar Studios, 59e59 Off-Broadway and UK Tour); assistant director of *Describe the Night* (Hampstead Theatre) and *The Majority* (National Theatre); and running Zut Alors Theatre.

Set and Costume Designer | David Allen
David is a London based Set and Costume designer working across theatre and live music productions. He trained in architecture before training in design for performance at Royal Welsh College of Music and Drama.
As Associate Designer – theatre credits include: *Cabaret* (Kit Kat Club at the Playhouse); *Mary Seacole* (Donmar Warehouse); *Jesus Christ Superstar, Little Shop of Horrors, Carousel* (Regent's Park); *Summer and Smoke* (Almeida); *A Very Expensive Poison* (Old Vic); *Fairview* (Young Vic); *The Deep Blue Sea* (National).
As Designer – theatre credits include: *Lonely Planet* (Trafalgar Studios).
As Art Director – other credits include: *Ben Platt Live from Radio City Music Hall; Christine and the Queens - Apple Music Live at Salle Pleyel; MTV Unplugged* (Live at Hull City Hall).
As Associate Designer – credits include: Pet Shop Boys Dreamworld tour.

Lighting Designer | Joe Price
Joe trained at the Royal Welsh College of Music & Drama, and was the recipient of the 2015 Francis Reid Award for Lighting Design.
Credits include: *My Name Is Rachel Corrie* (Young Vic); *Outlier* (Bristol Old Vic); *Petula* (National Theatre Wales); *The World's Wife* (Welsh National Opera); *Redefining Juliet* (Barbican); *Five Children And It, Rapunzel* (The Egg, TRB); *Revealed* (Tobacco Factory Theatres); *Heads Will Roll* (Told by an Idiot); *Heather* (Bush Theatre); *Quality Street* (Northern Broadsides); *Bitcoin Boi* (Riverfront Newport); *The Turn of the Screw* (RWCMD); *Ask Me Anything, Goldfish Bowl* (Paper Birds); *Kite* (UK & China Tour), *Conditionally* (Soho Theatre); *Mrs Dalloway, Carmen, How To Date A Feminist* (Arcola Theatre); *Fossils* (Brits off Broadway, NYC); *What Songs May Do* (Dance City); *Box Clever, Killymuck, Breathe* (Bunker Theatre); *Merboy* (Omnibus Theatre); *Peter Pan* (Barn Theatre); *Let the Right One In* (Arts Ed); *Magnificence, A Third* (Finborough Theatre); *Some Girl(s)* (Park Theatre); *Y Twr* (Invertigo).

Sound Designer and Composer | Hugh Sheehan

Hugh Sheehan is a musician – multi-instrumentalist, composer, sound designer, producer – from Birmingham, now based between the UK and Finland. He has equal footings in traditional Irish music and contemporary classical music, and the coalescence of these two worlds is supplemented by an adolescence spent in guitar bands and a continued preoccupation with club culture and electronic music. Much of his work is concerned with questions of sexuality and gender. In 2020 he was commissioned by BBC Arts and Arts Council England to make an audio work for their New Creatives series. In 2022 he was commissioned by The Sunday Boys and Melo'Men through Institut Français's fund for contemporary music to write a large-scale new work for low-voice choir and accordion.

Theatre highlights include: Plain Heroines' *SCRATCHES* by Aoife Kennan (Vault Festival and Arcola Theatre); *The 4th Country* by Kate Reid (Park Theatre); Rachel De-lahay's *The Hole* with NYT (The Old Rep); Lucy Roslyn's *Pennyroyal* (Finborough Theatre).

Associate Director and Movement Director | Sam Hooper

Sam is a 2011 graduate of the VCA Bachelor of Music Theatre, where he was awarded the Cassidy Bequest Scholarship in his graduating year. In 2018, he returned to the VCA to complete his honours project "The development and enhancement of movement narrative in live theatre".

Directing credits include: *Bonnie and Clyde* (Hayes Theatre Co); *1&Only* (VAULTS); *In Loving Memory* (Hayes Theatre Co); *A Chorus Line* (Bird College); *City of Angels* (Hayes Theatre Co); *Catch Me If You Can* (OCPAC); *They're Playing Our Song* (Company 11).

Assistant Directing: *Lipstick: A Fairytale of Modern Iran* (Omnibus Theatre); *The Apologists* (UK tour); *BARE* (Bird College); *The Drowsy Chaperone* (VCA); *Third World Blues* (Company 11).

Choreography: *Urinetown* (OCPAC); *Dreamsong* (VCA).

Writing: *Death Suits You* (WINNER: Show of the week, *VAULTS*; (WINNER: Spirit of the Fringe, Edinburgh Fringe)

Casting Director | Nadine Rennie CDG

Nadine has over twenty years' experience as a Casting Director for Theatre. She was in-house Casting Director at Soho Theatre for over fifteen years; working on new plays by writers including Dennis Kelly, Bryony Lavery, Arinzé Kene, Roy Williams, Philip Ridley, Laura Wade, Hassan Abdulrazzak, Phoebe Waller-Bridge and Oladipo Agboluaje. Since going freelance in January 2019, Nadine has worked for theatres and companies across London and the UK; including Arcola Theatre, Orange Tree Theatre, Sheffield Theatres, Leeds Playhouse, Paines Plough, Fuel Theatre, National Theatre of Wales, Northern Stage, Wales Millennium Centre, Kiln Theatre, Park Theatre, Theatre503, Pleasance Theatre London, Almeida, Lyric, Hampstead and Minack theatres. She continues to cast on a regular basis for Soho Theatre and has a long running relationship with Synergy Theatre Project as their Casting Director/ Consultant.

TV work includes: *Dixi* (BAFTA win, CBBC), casting the first three series. Nadine is a member of the Casting Directors Guild and currently sits on the Committee.

Stage Manager | Rose Hockaday
Rose Hockaday (she/her) is a Freelance Stage Manager based in London. **Theatre credits include:** *LORENZO* (2023 Fringe First winner), *Jali, Spellbound: Suhani Shah, Age Is A Feeling* (2022 Fringe First winner and 2023 Olivier Award nominee); *and Bedu* (Soho Theatre); *Worth* (New Earth); *Evita Too* (Sh!t Theatre); *harmony.* 天人合一, *At Broken Bridge, and No Particular Order* (Ellandar); *The Ex-Boyfriend Yard Sale* (London & Toronto); *Milk & Gall, Spiderfly, Wolfie, and Art of Gaman* (Theatre503); *Antigone*; *Pops*; *You Only Live Forever* & *In Tents and Purposes* (Viscera Theatre); *Timmy*; *Glitter Punch*; *How To Survive A Post-Truth Apocalypse*; *They Built It. No One Came* & *Jericho Creek (Fledgling Theatre)*.
Film credits include: *Heaven Knows, Visitors, Ignite, Pomegranate, Wandering Eyes,* and *Versions of Us.*
Music video credits include: "Phase Me Out", "When You're Gone", and "Saint" for artist VÉRITÉ.

Assistant Stage Manager On Placement | Amie Whickman
Amie is currently in her final year of studying Stage Management and Technical Theatre at the Royal Central School of Speech and Drama and is thrilled to be involved in this production at Theatre503!
Previous work includes: Deputy Stage Manager on *Hamlet* (Coutyard Theatre); Assistant Stage Manager on *Curtains the Musical* (Embassy Theatre); Technical Assistant Stage Manager on *Electra* (Webber Douglas Studio); Assistant Stage Manager on *Two Gentlemen of Verona* (Embassy Theatre). Amie is very grateful to have been given this opportunity to refine her skills alongside such professionals.

Production Manager | Misha Mah
Misha is a freelance Production Manager based in London.
Credits include: Housemates Festival 2023 (Brixton House); *How To Succeed In Business Without Really Trying* (Big Con Productions, Southwark Playhouse); *Sugar Coat* (Emma Blackman Productions, Southwark Playhouse); *Flies* (Boundless Theatre, Shoreditch Town Hall); *Brilliant Jerks* (RJG Productions, Southwark Playhouse); *Smoke* (3 hearts canvas, Southwark Playhouse); *Zombiegate* (Ameena Hamid Productions, Theatre503); *A Gig For Ghosts* (45North, Soho Theatre); *Far Gone* (Roots Mbili, ZOO Southside); *Caste-ing* (Nouveau Riche, Roundabout); *Hungry* (Paines Plough, Soho Theatre & Roundabout); *Kabul Goes Pop: Music Television Afghanistan* (Brixton House, Touring); *Til Death Do Us Part* (Theatre503).

Producer | Ceri Lothian

Ceri started her career as Resident Assistant Producer at Theatre503, working on new writing productions that included the World Premieres of *And Then Come The Nightjars* by Bea Roberts (2016 National Tour), and *Rotterdam* by Jon Brittain (Olivier Award Winner, 2017). She was Associate Producer & General Manager at Deus Ex Machina Productions from 2016-2021, where credits include *RIDE* (Garrick Theatre, 2021); *The Secret Diary of Adrian Mole Age 13 3/4: The Musical* (Ambassadors Theatre, 2019); *DUST* by Milly Thomas (Trafalgar Studio 2 2018, New York Theatre Workshop, 2019); *Spring Awakening* (Hope Mill Theatre, 2018); Stephen Schwartz' *Working* (Southwark Playhouse, 2017). She is currently the Producer at Theatre503, where credits include *Milk & Gall*, *Moreno*, and *The Boys Are Kissing*. Ceri has taken part in Stage One workshops, and is an Ambassador for Inspiring The Future of Theatre with SOLT and UK Theatre.

ACKNOWLEDGMENTS

This play has been bouncing around in my head for a while now, so it's really thanks to the following people that it's finally here.

Thanks to Sarah Sigal and Melli Marie, who supported the earliest workshops of this idea at JW3 and the Park Theatre's Script Accelerator Scheme respectively – and continued to check in even after I'd packed up and left.

The writing process began in a workshop but ended in lockdown. Thanks to Kate Handford, Jess Clark and Pedro Leandro for getting it up on its feet when I got stuck. And to everyone who read and gave notes, in particular Josh Roche, Lily Shahmoon, Claire Russell, David Overend, Kate Reid, Lucy Arditti, Donnacadh O'Briain, and Ed Eales-White. And in particular *in particular* Amy Tobias.

Thanks to everyone at the Women's Prize for Playwriting, Bruntwood Prize and especially Gill Greer at the Verity Bargate Award. All those votes of confidence really helped.

Then suddenly the play becomes a reality! Thanks to everyone involved in the award – 503 team, readers and judges. Huge thanks to Steven Greenhalgh, Charlie Coulthard and everyone at Concord for putting it on paper and being so incredibly supportive from day one. Thanks to Philip and Christine Carne for backing this award and backing new writing.

It's been really special to return to Theatre503 with this play. I was first here with Jon Brittain's *Rotterdam* – one of the loveliest jobs in one of the loveliest venues. Thanks to the whole team – Jade Lewis, Jules Oakshett, Emily Carewe, Emily Dickson, Lauretta Barrow. In particular Steve Harper for calmly and confidently helping me get the script up to scratch. And Lisa Spirling for being so positive and encouraging over the last six months. Lisa listened to what this play needed and adapted the process to suit it. I'm so grateful you trusted me to direct it – fingers crossed no regrets.

I've been away for a few years working in TV (soz) and so I've forgotten how productions come together in such a brilliantly chaotic and collaborative way.

Thanks to Frank Herfort for lending us his gorgeous photograph *Babushka* and Amelia Leuzzi for her graphic design and being the kindest, most talented person I know. David Ralf from Theatre Deli for stepping in to save the day more than once. A lot of organisations say they support artists – Deli really does.

We're yet to enter rehearsals and I already feel so hashtag blessed to have the team around me that I do. Thanks to my design boys David Allen, Hugh Sheehan and Joe Price for coming on this journey with me. And to our incredible cast - Sam Newton, Giulia Innocenti and Keith Dunphy – and the inimitable Nadine Rennie for finding them. Thanks also to Misha Mah, Nancy Poole, Humnah Abdullah, Amie Whickman and Rose Hockaday.

Special thanks to Sam Hooper, who was attached to this play at the Park Theatre, and who I haven't been able to shake loose since. I'm so glad you've stayed on this journey, and that your years working on *CATS* have finally paid off. And Ceri Lothian, truly the producer of dreams.

Lastly, this play would not be in the shape it is without Ben Mann and Alexandra Wetherell. Two brilliant actors who gave up a lot of their time to workshop it with me, and who originated some of the very best ideas.

Thanks to m&d for your unwavering support. I was scared to show this to you for a long time, but when I did you fully backed it. And gave me lots of notes. Toby, who hasn't ever read it, but enthusiastically booked a ticket to closing night. Celia, for everything, but mainly for reminding me that "it's just a play, Roxy" more than once.

Giulia said to me when we met – the storyteller in this play is the granddaughter. This is her trying to figure out how she feels about the old woman. I tried to act casj at the time, but I know now that she was right. Thanks to my Russian family. Those who will know about the play, and those who can't. Спасибо.

– Roxy Cook

For Babushka

ACT ONE

Scene One

Two storytellers address the audience.

A. A woman walks into a bank

B. An *old* woman walks into a bank

A. An old woman walks into a bank in Moscow, Russia because she'd seen a new sign on the window of the bank the week before that said

B. "Make your one day happen today"

With a picture of a man, who looked friendly, holding out money and smiling

A. And although, at the time, the old woman had thought nothing of the sign but just waited for the lights beside the bank to turn from red to green

B. Crossed the road

Gone home

A. She noticed the sign the next day and the next day and the next, until eventually it was one of the only things that had happened that week that she could remember

B. "Make your one day happen today"

Make today happen one day

One perfect nondescript day happening finally, brilliant, amazing

B. What happens tomorrow? Doesn't matter, your one day happened /

A. Okay.

And so, although the old woman wasn't entirely sure what the new sign meant or even referred to, she felt good about the man with the money and the smile, and so carried him around with her for the rest of the week, round the supermarket and the pharmacy and the boulevard, and even thought about him that evening as she prepared tea for herself, and for her cat

B. Sally.

(Beat.)

A woman walks into a bank

A. An old woman walks into a bank

B. An old woman walks into a bank in Moscow, Russia because she needs money again

And she needs money because old women in Russia always need money

A. This is common knowledge

B. Free trips to the Black Sea if your father was tortured in the gulag, sure

But money?

Nah

A. No, she needs money again because earlier that week she'd telephoned her daughter

B. A translator

A. Who lives abroad with her foreign family, somewhere foreign

B. And she'd said

A. "I need money

I need money so I can buy food for myself, and food for Sally, and medicine for me, and presents for you"

B. And her daughter had, like many times before, sat at her desk, opened her laptop, transferred the money, phoned the old woman back, told her she'd transferred it, and then returned to her translating and her family somewhere far away, somewhere foreign

A. And the old woman had gone to the machine, taken out a portion of the money and gone home

B. And she'd done the same thing the next day

A. And the next

B. And the next

A. And the next

B. Until on the fifth day she'd taken out all of the money

All five portions

Put it in a box

And put it away

A. Far away at the top of her wardrobe, far away from the bank across the road.

(Beat. **B** *is confused.)*

B. So an old woman walks into a bank because an old woman doesn't trust banks?

A. Well no, she just likes to have something she can

It's just what she's always done

She's used rubles since Stalin was in power, and now you expect her to trust a number on a screen? No and thank you!

B. Okay.

(Beat. **B** *is still confused.)*

B. So an old woman walks into a bank in Moscow, Russia because she has money in her apartment already?

A. But she's forgotten where it is

B. Riiiiiight

A. And not only that

But she's forgotten about her trips to the machine, the box, the wardrobe, and so she thinks, she *decides*

If my daughter can't follow through with her promises, if she can't even do that, then I'll have to find someone else who can

B. And just as she thinks this, she looks out of the window at the bank across the road and yes!

The man with the smile, holding out some money

A. Of course.

(Beat. Gorgeous tranquility.)

An old woman walks into a bank and is surprised by just how calm everything is

B. How quiet and still, no traffic, no voices

A. A different world

B. Squares of teal and green spin out in pleasing diagonals

A. A television plays quietly

News, improvements, seating in the park

B. Men and women nod in appreciation

A. And other men and women talk quietly behind screens

B. And a man takes out money in a

Reassuring way

A. An old woman feels a calm, a clarity

And as she stands there, just for a moment, for the first moment in a very long time, she finds something

B. A lifting mist

A. And she thinks, she thinks...

(A lightbulb moment.)

That money is at the top of my wardrobe, in that nice box Svetlana gave me!

She remembers, she turns, she walks out of the bank /

B. Except

That at that precise moment

A. She's actually still in the bank

B. At that precise moment of clarity, of calm

A. A young man spots her

B. Jumps up

A. Touches her on the shoulder and says

B. "Can I help you, Gran?"

A. And so an old woman forgets all about the box and the wardrobe and says "Yes".

Scene Two

Unapologetic, unfiltered exuberance.

B. A young man walks up to an old woman

A. A young man walks up to an old woman who has just walked into a bank

B. A young man does this

All these things you've probably grasped by now

Because he is EXCITED

A. And he is excited because he has recently become

'The Bank Manager'!

B. That's right

He's twenty-five, only twenty-five, but after three years of working at the bank, they've realised what he realised so long ago

That like most great men in Russia

He has a work ethic like no other

An authority that is commanding but doesn't make you feel like you're being put in your place

A sort of je ne sais /

A. Okay, okay

Let's just

A young man *does* walk up to an old woman in a bank in Moscow Russia

But he's one of *three* bank managers

B. One of three managers who were recently told that they were being promoted!

A. Or that their job titles were being changed

Internally

B. And although the woman telling them this didn't go into the exact details of why or how or who came up with the idea

She *did* talk about

A. "A new initiative to build confidence in employees and confidence in clients!"

B. "Want to speak to the manager?

I'm here

I can help

Young? Sure, but did you see my badge?"

A. He's not really a manager, he doesn't manage anything

And the young man does know all this, he does

B. Buuuuut

He knows it and then he forgets it

A. He forgets it because really, when you break it down to everyone outside the bank

B. Mum at home

A. Mum's friends round for tea

B. Dad on the phone

A. Girls from school who he never spoke to but might bump into one day

B. The guy sweeping the pavement outside the bank watching him walk in every morning with his name badge on

A. To all those people he really is

'The Bank Manager'

B. He did well at school

A. But never in the *right* ways, you know?

B. He was teased for having a baby face

A. He was teased for having a dad from somewhere else

B. He was teased by the kids at the bottom for not being at the bottom and the kids at the top for not being at at the top

A. And so now it's his moment and he is excited

B. He's allowed to be excited

He's 'The Bank Manager', so who the fuck cares?

> *(Beat.)*

A. A young man walks up to an old woman in a bank in Moscow, Russia /

B. Because we're in Russia, did we mention that it's August 2018 and that we are in Russia?

We're in Russia and there's this buzz, like this buzz going round

We just hosted the World Cup

A. The *incident-free* World Cup

B. And everyone had a great time

A. There was free Metro travel

B. Parties in the square

A. The police, the ones with guns, they were smiling

B. Did we mention it was an incident-free event?

A. And…

We got to the Quarter Finals!

> *(They celebrate.)*

B. It all seems a little distant now but people finally saw that

Yeah, it's actually okay over here, and no, it doesn't snow in the summer, it's actually very warm

A. And okay we're a little confident, we get that, but it's just because we really are

Better

B. Despite everything we have been through

We are

Better

Think of like a sport, or an art form maybe

Got one got one GOT ONE?

A. Theatre!

B. We invented it

Okay we didn't invent it, but we took what it had been before and we made it our own

Shakespeare, great, you can keep him

But the minutiae of everyday behaviour?

Compelling psychological reality?

Is it comedy

Is it tragedy

A. It's the Russian soul, that's what it is!

> *(Their cockiness takes a sinister turn. This could involve an audience member.)*

B. We just have this thing

You don't want to admit it's true

But it absolutely *is* true, and the funny thing is, everybody knows it

A. This young man is excited and we're excited, we're excited *for* him

A. Who cares if he's not really a bank manager

B. His name badge says bank manager, he feels like a bank manager

So let him enjoy this moment

A. It's 2018

B. We're in Russia!

> *(Beat.)*

A young man walks up to an old woman in Moscow, Russia because of all these things

A. But mainly because the rules have changed

B. Again

A. And that along with calling twenty-five-year-old losers bank managers, the bank has also introduced an initiative to get pensioners to sign up to loans

B. Pensioners who don't have someone there to say

A. Maybe...not?

B. And these loans are quick, they are easy

A. A special offer for a special Babushka!

B. "Make your one day happen today"

A. But they also have reaaaally big interest rates

B. Interest rates you only find out about when your bank sells your loan to a debt collector

A. And the debt collector starts charging you two percent interest a day

B. That's seven hundred and thirty percent interest a year

A. Not sure how that's legal

B. But it *is* legal.

> *(Beat.)*

A. A young man walks up to an old woman in a bank in Moscow, Russia because there's this initiative, these loans, but

> (**B**'s *bravado begins to dwindle.*)

B. He hasn't sold one yet

He's just not found the right time to, you know

He's trying to gage the, before

Yeah

A. The bank understands

B. The bank seems to understand

A. No one's told him something bad will happen if he doesn't sell a loan

B. But also

A. No one's told him something bad *won't* happen if he doesn't sell a loan.

> (*Beat. The storytellers start wrapping up, each in their own way.*)

B. And so a young man walks up to an old woman because she seems to be standing, waiting for him /

A. And then she turns, like she's suddenly realised she's in the wrong building, and leaves

Gone

And actually

Surprisingly

He feels relieved.

> (*Beat.* **B** *realises what's just happened.*)

B. No he doesn't, he doesn't feel relieved

B. "I'm so relieved" said no Russian ever!

No, she turns but she hasn't left yet

And so he jumps up, touches her on the shoulder and says

"Can I help you, Gran?" and /

A. Her grey eyes cloud over

And in that momentary shade he sees his dear Granny Irina who he loves very, very much

And he /

B. No, no, he doesn't

His granny isn't called Irina, she's called *Da*rina

And she doesn't have grey eyes, she has dark eyes, like him, no

He jumps up, touches her on the shoulder and says

"Can I help you, Gran?"

A. And her eyes /

B. *Do* cloud over

But he doesn't look away this time

He just smiles

And then she smiles too and says

A. "Yes."

Scene Three

The storytellers sit, and as the scene progresses become more and more cat-like.

B. A cat

Sits in a balcony room on the fifth floor of an apartment block in Moscow, Russia

A. The cat is called Sally

Sally is eighteen years old

Which is old

B. Sally is brown

A. *Tabby*

B. Sally has green eyes

A. Sally is prone to scratching people she doesn't know

Sally is prone to scratching people she does know

Sally is

Temperamental

B. Sure

A. But today Sally is worried

As worried as a cat called Sally can really be

B. Sally is worried because the old woman she shares her apartment with left suddenly and hasn't come back

Sally's not a needy cat, no, Sally is fine being alone

In fact Sally would rather be alone, thank you very much

But

A. There's a routine

A. What you've come to expect

Certain rituals and rules and ways of doing things

And this is…

B. A deviation.

> *(Beat.)*

A. And there's something else

That's worrying

B. Yes

A. The old woman has started feeding her three times a day instead of two

B. Sally doesn't mind

I mean, you know

A. But the thing is

The thing is

B. Sally's noticed that she's getting a little bit

Fat?

A. Because if you give Sally food

Sally *will* eat it

B. Like, she's a cat

A. And so this deviation

B. This

Deviation

A. Is worrying.

Scene Four

The storytellers perform the transaction, and in doing so begin to take on more distinct roles. **A**, *the old woman and* **B**, *the young man.*

B. A young man walks an old woman over to a blue plastic chair and he is excited

A. His name badge, fantastic, yes

B. But what does it even mean?

It's not real

Wait, you know it's not actually real, right?

A. There's being a bank manager and then there's like

Being

A bank manager

B. Waiting for the right moment

A. Seizing that opportunity

B. Nodding to your colleagues as you bring the new client over to the

New

Client

Area

A. Using the branded pens cause you've got something to write this time

Thinking

B. *Fuck*

This suit fits well

A. There's being a bank manager and then there's saying

B. "Alright Gran

Now let's get you sorted."

*(Beat. We move to **A**, an old woman.)*

A. An old woman sits down in a blue plastic chair and she is excited

Banks aren't scary

B. They've never been scary!

A. And it's unfortunate she found this out so late

B. Family member tell you otherwise?

A. Avoided them for so long

B. People love a good story

A. But she's here now

With this nice young man with a smile

B. And some money!

A. She's making it happen, today

Finally.

*(Beat. We move to **B**, a young man.)*

B. A young man sits in a blue plastic chair and he is excited.

(Beat.)

He is excited but he is also worried

He is worried because the old woman keeps asking him the same questions over and over again like

A. "How long have you worked here?"

B. And

A. "What's your name then?"

B. And then again

A. "What's your name?"

B. And the bank did mention this might happen

And they did even role play a scenario where this might happen

And he wants to sell a loan he really does but not to anyone, okay, there are *some* lines that you have to draw

And like most great men in Russia, he knows that those lines are important.

> *(Beat. We move to* **A,** *an old woman.)*

A. An old woman sits in a blue plastic chair because

An old woman sits in a blue plastic chair in a bank in Moscow, Russia because

Because...

I don't

> *(***A*** looks around, at* **B** *and at the audience, as if she's never seen them before.)*

She doesn't remember what the form is for

She doesn't even remember filling out the first half of the form

B. But it *is* her handwriting

And the handwriting *is* still wet

And there *is* a young man sitting opposite her smiling

A. He has a kind face, a baby face

A face you don't see so much anymore

B. And there's a television playing, good news, improvements in the square

A. And men and women nod in appreciation

And other men and women murmur behind screens

B. And so?

A. An old woman, not wanting to trouble him, not wanting to trouble anyone

Continues filling out the form

No cause for alarm.

(Beat. We move to **B**, *a young man.)*

B. A young man sits in a blue plastic chair in a bank in Moscow, Russia and he looks at an old woman, and he looks at his colleagues standing, watching behind the glass, and he feels...

Better

Sure, she asked him the same thing once or twice

But look, she remembers all the important stuff

She knows what she's doing!

And if she doesn't know what she's doing, then whose fault is that?

(They both stand up suddenly.)

A. And then she's done

She signs it

Gives it back

B. And he takes her to his colleague behind the glass

A. And it is so simple

B. So incredibly simple

A & B. We're really surprised that there isn't more to it

B. But just as he's leaving, just as he turns around and walks away

She touches him on the shoulder and says

A. "Thank you, you were very helpful"

B. Fuck.

> *(A flicker of guilt.)*

A. And he?

B. He goes to the canteen across the road and orders three things!

Why not?

Today has been a good day

Today has been an exceptionally good day

Today has been an exceptionally good day, particularly when you compare it to all the underwhelming days he's had

"Make your one day happen"

Too right!

Scene Five

Cat-like again.

A. A cat called Sally continues to sit alone in a balcony room in Moscow, Russia

B. She's played with her ball

A. She's done some scratching

B. She's played with her mouse

Even though Sally does know

A. She does

B. That it's not a real mouse

Sally's not stupid

A. But

Winning feels good

B. And so now, Sally might as well nap

A. She's not just going to throw all her plans out the window because the old woman she shares her apartment with hasn't come back

Is she?

B. She's not

A. And so

She goes to look for somewhere to nap

Somewhere

Rectangular

B. Yes

Somewhere

Rectangular.

> *(Beat. The storytellers begin to look around the space.)*

A. What about /

B. No

> *(B spots somewhere.)*

That's always looked comfy

A. Do you remember the last time she cleaned it?

> *(A spots somewhere.)*

There?

B. Where?

A. *There*

B. Perfect

A. Lightly

B. She is

A. Lightly

B. She

Jesus!

What's that?

A. A pine cone

A *decorative* pine cone

She stepped on it yesterday

B. Do you blame her?

How is Sally supposed to navigate this mess?

A. Okay but look

B. Yes?

A & B. Yes!

(Beat.)

B. A box at the top of the old woman's wardrobe

Whose door she has

A. For all her flaws

B. Rather kindly

Left ajar

A. And this box is

Perrrrrfect

B. Because as well as being rectangular, it has lots of little bundles of coloured paper in it

Each one beautifully decorated with one of Sally's favourite historical landmarks

A. Sally can definitely work with this

B. And so she gets in, curls up,

And falls asleep.

Scene Six

A refresh in energy.

A. Now

Somewhere else in Moscow, Russia

B. Somewhere completely totally one hundred percent else in Moscow, Russia

A. A debt collector sits in a warehouse in a suburb of a suburb of a /

B. Wait

A *Russian* debt collector sits in an warehouse in a suburb of a suburb of a suburb

There's a difference, remember?

(**A** *can't disagree with this.*)

And so this Russian debt collector

Ivan?

A. He says his name is Ivan, but so do most of them

That guy, two desks away

Ivan

B. This blonde one with the funny moustache

Also Ivan!

A. The man making calls in the corner while he smokes a cigarette and lights another with his spare hand?

B. You've guessed it

Ivan!

A. They all use fake names here

B. They're not literally all called Ivan

A. But for all of you, right now

Their real names don't matter

B. It's what they do that matters.

(Beat. Super fun presentation mode GO!)

A. A young woman opens the door of her apartment one morning to find the word "THIEF" spray-painted on the name plate

B. Just in case the neighbours were wondering

A. An old man reads his grandson a bedtime story

B. As a molotov cocktail comes flying through the window

A. And this guy in the East

B. You must have heard this one

A. Opens the paper one morning to find an obituary for his one-year-old daughter

B. She is alive and well

A. But now all he can think about is whether she'll always be alive and well

B. There's a checklist

A

Cheat sheet if you will

A. And this Russian debt collector knows it.

(Beat.)

B. He knows that you start by calling repeatedly

A. Not repeatedly

Incessantly

Hundreds of times a day

B. And if that doesn't work

Call the parents

A. No parents?

No problem!

Children are a more...

B. *Rewarding*

A. Target

        (**C** *enters.* **A** *and* **B** *don't notice him.*)

B. Scratch the car

A. Glue the locks

B. Steal the pets

A. And if none of that works, if literally not a single one of those things work

B. Accuse them of being a paedophile

A. It *is* a classic

In Russia

C. Okay so some guy, somewhere in Russia

Not sure where, it *is* quite big

Goes rogue

But does it have anything to do with him?

        (*Beat.* **A** *and* **B** *are shocked – they do not know who* **C** *is or what he's doing here.*)

B. Er

A. Well

B. I suppose it depends on who *he* is

A. And on what *he's* doing here

Sorry, did I miss something, who exactly is he?

C. A debt collector

You just

B. Okay, but we're getting into it

Providing some context for the world he

C. Me?

B. Is from

C. Moscow, Russia?

And so this debt collector

Who *is* called Ivan by the way

Goes outside to eat the lunch that his wife Olga made him that morning.

(*An awkward beat.*)

B. I'm sorry

Let's just

Ivan

C. Yes?

A. He's not called Ivan!

B. Why is his lunch relevant?

And who is Olga?

C. His wife

B. No, I get it but

"A debt collector eats his lunch"!

C. Vinegret

The classic Russian salad

I mean we have a lot of classics but this is a real classic

A worker's lunch

An old time favourite

And Olga makes the best vinegret

Potatoes, carrots, pickled cabbage, peas and onion

Nothing from the ground will hurt you

Beetroot because

We're in Russia, you don't need a reason

And lashings of pickled cucumber

For the soul.

(Another awkward beat.)

A. Can we just go back a bit?

A debt collector sits in an warehouse and his phone /

(Sharply.)

C. Not yet

He has ten minutes

Just let him have ten

B. Okay?

A. Okay?!

B. What do you want me to

A debt collector sits in an warehouse

Sorry

A debt collector goes *outside*

To a courtyard surrounded by flats?

C. Flats that rise high

Protecting it

B. Protecting a playground with benches and a fountain and a

Kiosk?

C. Yes

A. A kiosk that sells surprisingly good pastries?

C. Not surprisingly

Everyone knows that the best pastries come from kiosks in courtyards

Look at it

(**A** *and* **B** *look. They begin to buy into it.*)

Still and

Warm

And the only sound, the only movement

Little black birds

B. Sparrows maybe?

C. Jumping in and out of the fountain

Shaking themselves dry

B. It is so still

A. And it is so peaceful

C. You can just

(*They breathe in deeply – feel his spell on them.*)

A. And yes

He thinks

There *are* birds washing themselves in fountains in courtyards all over Moscow

C. But who cares?

These are my birds

This is my courtyard

This is my modern Russian scene

A. And so this /

C. Man

Free to be

Just a man

A. Joins the birds and rinses the lunchbox Olga gave him

B. And then he goes to the kiosk where a young woman sits everyday

C. He likes her

A. Buys a magazine for Olga and cigarettes for himself

B. Sits on a bench and smokes

A. And just as he thinks this couldn't get anymore

C. You know when you have moments like that?

A. Music

(A traditional Russian tune plays softly.)

C. Russian music

The *best* kind of music

A song he's loved since he was small

B. And he doesn't worry about why it's playing

In a courtyard

At lunchtime

C. He just listens as it grows

B. Gently at first

A. Then bigger

C. Grander

B. Louder

A. Until his phone

*(As the song becomes a jarring ringtone, **C**
realises what **A** and **B** are doing.)*

C. No

A. His phone

C. No

B. His phone

C. No no

You bastards!

B. His phone buzzing angrily in his pocket

A. What's this about a modern Russian scene?

Wake the fuck up!

> (**C** *picks up.*)

C. "What?"

A. "What do you mean what?

This is the third time I've called you"

B. "Is your phone broken or should I be concerned?"

C. "No

Lunch"

A. "I don't care which meal you're eating

If I call you, you pick up the phone"

C. "I"

B. "Whatever, just

Get a pen"

A. "New moocher".

> (*Beat. Everything falls apart.*)

C. And it's broken just like that

A. The young woman in the kiosk frowns

C. She's never frowned before!

B. The birds fly to a courtyard somewhere else

A. And this man who is no longer just a man free to eat his lunch

B. Oh how idyllic!

A. But a debt collector, remember?

C. Fine

B. He?

C. Leaves a courtyard that is quiet and peaceful because the only people who rent spaces there

B. An experimental theatre company

A. A children's charity

B. Have to be quiet

A. Have to be peaceful

C. And hurries back to the warehouse, phone still cursing in his hand

A. "I don't understand why this is taking so long"

C. Takes the pen his wife Olga

B. Who probably doesn't make the best vinegret

She just makes it, she doesn't master it

C. Bought him for their anniversary last year

And writes down the information about

A. "An old woman who walked into a bank this morning because she needed money"

C. Or at least that's what they've told her

B. "Who has until the end of September to pay it back"

C. That sounds realistic

A. "Who lives in Kutuzovsky"

C. Good for her

B. "Who has no named dependents"

C. Not inconceivable

A. "And who was born in 1936"

C. The same year as his mother.

> *(Beat. **C** is unsettled by this fact, but brushes it away.)*

And so a debt collector ends the call

Makes a note of when the money is due

And wonders if the old woman has done the same.

Scene Seven

> *Where were we?*

A. An old woman walks into a bank in Moscow, Russia

B. No, she doesn't

An old woman has already walked into a bank in Moscow, Russia

Remember?

A. Yes

Of course

It can get confusing.

> *(Beat.)*

B. An old woman walks into an *apartment*

C. An old woman walks into an apartment on the fifth floor of an apartment block?

B. An old woman walks into an apartment on the fifth floor of an apartment block with some money and some papers about when the money is due, and she knows

Like every Russian her age knows

That she needs to put them somewhere safe

A. Yes, very good

And so as she puts on her slippers, makes a cup of tea and thinks about somewhere safe to put them

She realises that she feels in control

You see, when you get older, no one takes you seriously

C. People just ask you how your back is

A. Worse

B. Or how your foot is

A. Worse

C. Or how your teeth are

A. What teeth?

C. And you can be in a whole room of people who know you and share the same blood as you

A. And have finally bothered to get on a plane to celebrate your eightieth birthday, whatever that really means

But even then, not one person will ask you a question

And then when you *do* say something, when you actually bother to say something, they tell you you're repeating yourself and you think

Of course I'm repeating myself you little shit, I'm repeating myself because your mother never taught you Russian, did she?

(Beat. B and C are not sure how to respond.)

B. Let's just

An old woman walks into an apartment

C. An old woman walks into an apartment on the fifth floor of an apartment block

B. And she sees

A wardrobe

A. I thought she was having tea in the kitchen?

B. Well she could be in her bedroom now, it's not a stretch

C. And

Yes!

She thinks

I'll put the money and the papers about when the money is due

B. That I'm holding

Right

Now

(**A** *realises that this is, indeed, the case.*)

A. Oh

C. At the top of my wardrobe, in that nice box Svetlana

A. The only person who bothered to stick around!

C. Gave me

A. Because the truth is, you see the truth is

She loves her daughter and her foreign family very much, but she also knows that she can't rely on her forever

I mean how can someone be there for you if they're not

Actually

There for you?

If they left when it got a little bit difficult

B. Hasn't it always been difficult?

A. Chose to raise their kids different

C. They're still Russian /

A. They're *not* Russian!

And so

B & C. And so?

A. An old woman knows that when there are no potatoes in the cupboard, you go out and you buy potatoes

When there are no potatoes in the shop, you go out and you plant potatoes

And when there is no soil, no water, no space to even grow a bloody potato

A. Then you knuckle down and accept that tonight you'll go hungry!

> *(Beat.)*

Where were we?

C. Er

A. An old woman walks into an apartment and she /

> *(**B** and **C** seize their opportunity and don't let go.)*

B. Sees her wardrobe, kindly ajar

A sign!

C. And there at the top, just like she remembers

B. That nice box

Svetlana!

C. But wait!

It's not empty like she thought, no, it's full of money, HER money, her money that her daughter

B. Despite having left, despite building a life in the West, despite having children who okay haven't mastered the language, the grammar's obscene

C. Sent her last week

B. Look

The receipt

> *(It all dawns on **A.**)*

A. Money

She already had money

C. And she realises that she probably needs to phone her daughter

B. That she probably needs to phone her doctor

C. That she probably needs to cross the road, go to the bank and pay back the loan immediately before /

A. No

B & C. No?

A. Maybe somewhere

Maybe later?

But not here, not now

Because an old woman *does* walk into an apartment and she *does* finally get round to opening a wardrobe

But at that precise moment

A cat!

C. There's a cat?

B. Fucking Sally

A. Jumps out

And so an old woman forgets all about the

> *(Struggling to remember what it is she's forgotten.)*

And goes to make Sally dinner.

Scene Eight

Cloud nine.

A. A young man

B. Did we mention that he's young?

A. Walks out of a bank.

> *(Beat.)*

C. A young man /

B. Sorry, shall we just call him what he is?

A motherfucking BANK manager walks out of a bank

His bank

It may as well be his bank

C. And starts his commute home

B. Think London is big?

Moscow

Is

Bigger

A. And so

It sucks

B. But not today

Today it tastes different

Today

As he swipes his Troika card

As he walks past the mosaic of Lenin looking out into the distance

As he presses against the person trying to get on the carriage thirty seconds sooner than him

There's meaning to his movement

C. There's meaning to everyone's movement

B. As they walk together, press together

They might be crammed into a Metro carriage okay we get that we do

But they are crammed in it

Together.

> *(Beat.)*

A. And so a bank manager stands in a Metro carriage

C. A bank manager stands in a *second* Metro carriage

A. A bank manager stands in a *third*

Are we going to stand in Metro carriages all /

B. As it emerges into his district in the South East of Moscow.

> *(Beat.* **A** *and* **C** *share a look – it is not the nice part.)*

And he thinks about how years from now, he will come back here

A. Here?

C. Are you sure?

B. Just to visit his mum

Just to see how she's doing

C. He won't *need* to be on the Metro, he'll have his own car

A. A driver too

B. But

He'll ride it anyway

B. He's still humble

A. And people will see him and say

C. "That's *her* son

The one I told you about

That's him"

B. That's me!

A. "Did you know that he became a bank manager at twenty-five

Only twenty-five

And did you know that almost immediately after becoming a bank manager he made a sale and got his first client"

B. It just fit, it made sense

Like

A. Rolling in the snow after the banya

C. Like a cool glass of kvass on a hot summer's day

B. Like pickle with your vodka, like /

A. He'll leave the Metro and he won't say anything

B. But he'll smile

A humble smile

C. And he'll walk up the streets that he used to know so well

B. And he'll buy his mother flowers

Yes, that's a nice touch

Maybe he'll buy her her *favourite* flowers

A. He doesn't know what they are /

B. Now

But he will then!

A. And no one in his district is selling anyone flowers

B. But they will then!

And she'll be so happy to see him

And they'll talk about today

And how he became the person he was always meant to be

The person he always /

C. No

B. / was.

     (Beat.)

C. A bank manager does walk up the hill to his housing complex, and he does walk through the maze of buildings to his indistinguishable own, and he does take the stairs, the elevator is broken, up to his apartment on the ninth floor of an apartment block

But

His mother isn't there

B. Oh

Really?

A. She starts her night shift now

C. She always starts her night shift now

B. He knows that

He just thought...

     (**B** *turns it around.*)

Fuck it

He is *still* excited

This is *still* exciting

B. And he knows that if you want someone to celebrate with, pat yourself on the back with, then you take out your phone and you send some fucking texts!

>   *(Beat.)*

A young man texts three friends

A. Three classmates he hasn't spoken to since they graduated and he asked for their numbers

B. "Ey Nik"

"Ey Pyotr"

"Ey Sash"

A. And then a fourth just in case

B. "Ey Anton, I'm bored, wanna get"

C. And then a beer emoji followed by a party popper emoji followed by a gif of someone throwing up.

>   *(A long beat. They wait for someone, anyone, to text back.)*

A. It has been thirty minutes and

C. Nothing

B. He chose carefully

He chose fucking carefully and not even Anton?

What is Anton doing?

A. But

He knows

B. It's a work night, okay fair enough

C. And he does know

B. He did text late

He didn't give any notice

I mean it *is* 2018 and we *are* in Russia!

(Another excruciating beat.)

C. Ninety minutes and still

(Nothing. The storytellers become restless.)

B. He takes a shower

A. He finishes the soup his mother's left him and then he does the washing up

B. He does ten pull ups on the bar above his bed

C. He does *two* pull ups on the bar above his bed and then he goes to the drink cabinet and gets out the good cognac his dad brought them last time he visited

B. They may be poor but you've got to have good cognac

A. And he pours himself a glass, puts the bottle away, and arranges it so the label is facing the same way

C. And then he pours himself another glass and puts the bottle away

B. And then he pours himself a third and a fourth glass and thinks well I'd better leave the bottle out, let's be realistic

His mum will understand

Every Russian understands that a toast

A. Even if you're alone in your apartment at nine o'clock on a Thursday night

B. Is still a goddamn toast.

(Beat. **B** *is drunk.)*

C. A young man drinks an entire bottle of cognac and he

Is

Smashed

*(***B*** *is full of self loathing.)*

B. He's Russian

He's STILL Russian!

A. But he's also STILL smashed

B. He has always hated the taste of spirits

C. Unfortunate

In Russia.

(*Beat.*)

A. And so as a young man sits alone

C. Smashed

B. He thinks about the old woman he sold the loan to and whether his dad would have done the same

If he would have walked up to her in the first place

C. If

When she asked him the same questions over and over again

A. "What's your name son?"

B. I

A. "What's your name then?"

B. Why

A. "What's your /"

B. I've already told you my name!

C. He would have seen that line

Straight and bold and blaring

Undeniable

Unambiguous

A. Screaming

You're on the wrong side of it

C. You *know* you're on the wrong side of it

A. And he feels...

B. He feels...

A. Tell us what he feels!

> *(Beat – guilt?)*

B. He feels his phone vibrate in his pocket!

A mash up of a Russian song he likes, it's a little corny but FUCK YES it's Pyotr!

A. No

B. Yes

A. No

B. Yes yes yes yes

It's Pyotr!

Look

C. "Haha Y E S cum 2 mine l8r"

Beer emoji vomit emoji

Gun emoji?

> *(Beat.)*

A. And so a young man

C. Absolutely smashed

B. I'll take this one

A BANK Manager with several solid drinks in him

A. Forgets all about his dad and the old woman and the line

B. It doesn't actually exist, it's just a metaphor

C. Puts on a silk shirt his mother bought him for his eighteenth birthday

B. It still fits!

A. It's a little tight

B. Hides the empty bottle of cognac in his wardrobe
And leaves the apartment.

Scene Nine

The end of another heavy day.

C. A debt collector arrives home to the Eastern district where he lives

B. And sees

A. In a neighbourhood where nothing is new

B. A single, shiny black car with a personalised number plate

C. His brother's car.

(Beat. **C** *tries to stay composed.)*

And so he decides to take the stairs

Keeps him healthy

A. Well, no

He never takes the stairs

B. And he's not really

Into health

A. But today he needs time to think

Why his brother

C. Who is never here

A. Is here

Why his brother

C. Who is always too busy to visit family

A. Is here

Why his /

C. Car dealing

C. Draft dodging

America loving

It's the nineties, everything we fought for is being forgotten but it doesn't matter it's a free for all brother

Is here

A. He's barely spoken to him since he said

B. "You lost your job, I'm sorry, it sucks

But I spoke to Dima and there's nothing I can do

He needs to invest in newbies

Kids he'll have for another ten, twenty years

Times are changing

The way things are done around here is changing

It's 2014

Have you noticed it's 2014?

It's not personal".

    (Beat.)

C. And so as a debt collector climbs the stairs he begins to

A. Panic?

C. Begins to *think*

Why his brother's here, but even weirder, unannounced?

Who's ill

Who's broke

Who died

A. And then, as he reaches the top

Realises that maybe

C. No, definitely

It's him they're all here for

(They know)

Or his brother found out and now the rest of them know.

> *(Beat.)*

B. Wait

A. Sorry

B. They don't know he's a debt collector?

C. A *Russian* debt collector

You said it yourself

A. Okay but

"What does it have to do with him?"

B. "They're just stories!"

C. Stories everyone knows.

> *(Beat.)*

And so he decides to just

Listen

He is good at this

He is an *expert* at this

A. He knows how to stand outside doors and count worried voices

B. Footsteps on floorboards

A. If there's anything he knows then it's /

C. Listen!

> *(They do.)*

C. A group of people

Six, maybe seven

B. Why are there six maybe seven people in his apartment?

A. Maybe they're going to take his stuff!

C. If he had any 'stuff', do you think he'd be doing this?

This isn't what he studied, served, worked hard in order to do

Standing in stairways

Listening.

(Beat.)

A. And so a debt collector, standing outside his own apartment door, eavesdropping on his own family inside

Wonders

B. What his sons

A. Mother

B. Brother

C. Olga

B. Would think if they found out he didn't work in security

C. He doesn't wonder because he knows

He's the one who taught them to go to church

A. Never miss gym

B. Be respectful of teachers

A. And soldiers

B. And ill people

A. And old people

C. And never spend more money than you have

There *will* be consequences

B. People you don't want after you

After you

A. People with no respect for the law

B. Telling you you've broken the law

C. You've heard the stories?

Guess what! They're not stories

He knows what they'll think because they're his and he told them

And they'll be

They'll be

Wait

Should he tell them?

A & B. "SURPRIIIIIISE!!!"

C. The door swings open

(*Beat.* **C** *is stunned.*)

Doors never swing open

A. But there they are

B. Sons

A. Mother

C. *Brother*

A. Olga

B. Aleks and Nastya

C. Why are Aleks and Nastya /

A. Here

Waiting

B. And smiling

C. For *him*?

> *(Beat.)*

A debt collector stands in the doorway of his apartment and it takes him a moment to realise what they've just said, and then they realise that he hasn't realised and murmur another quiet

A & B. "Surpriiiiiiiise"

A. And then that's it!

> *(Happy chaos.)*

C. And a debt collector who is no longer a debt collector

A. But a husband

B. Father

A. Son

B. Brother

A. Neighbour, oh he's an excellent neighbour!

B. An upstanding citizen

An Afghanistan veteran

A man working in an unnamed security firm, no questions asked!

C. Is pulled inside

> *(**A** and **B** play everyone – it doesn't need to be clear who, it's overwhelming and chaotic.)*

A. "We thought we heard you, what were you doing, did you know?"

B. "Happy birthday little brother

Don't worry, he's delighted!

I can see it in those eyes

Somewhere..."

A. "Never one for birthdays

Good day?"

C. His birthday?

Not for /

A. "It was the only day we could get everyone together"

B. "Q3's been mental"

A. "Can I get you a juice?"

B. "Why are you wearing this jacket, it's absolutely boiling!"

A. "Say hello to Aleks, did you say hello to Aleks?

B. "I think he's surprised

Come see what we did"

   (Beat.)

C. A debt collector walks into the living room and sees his kitchen table, modest once, now

Glorious

Squeezed between the TV and couch and covered in food

So much food

A. Herring

B. Eggs stuffed with caviar

A. Cabbage pies

B. Potato pies

C. She's not got much to say Nastya, but at some point some genius taught her to make delicious pies

B. Olivier salad

Beetroot salad

A & B. Vinegret!

C. Olga

How did she?

A. But Olga just smiles and nods at his brother

B. Who leans over and winks

C. Why does he always fucking wink?

B. And then raises his glass, looks him straight in the eye and says

"A toast!"

Scene Ten

Frenzy.

A. A young man stands in a queue for a Moscow nightclub he's heard of but never been to and he is excited

B. How could he not be?

Moscow is known for its nightclubs

You might never have heard of them before but trust me, Moscow is known for its nightclubs

There's a reason it's difficult to get a visa here LISTEN

Before 1991 there wasn't a single nightclub here, not a single one

Think of it as day one, the beginning of time

But since then since then HUNDREDS

Forget Berlin

Forget New York

Forget fucking St Petersburg

C. Especially forget fucking St Petersburg

(They all spit.)

B. Because you can have a good time there, you can have a nice time there but

Is a nice time really what you're after?

In Moscow you can have a life changing experience

We know how to spend money when we've got it!

(Beat.)

A. A young man stands in the queue for a Moscow nightclub and he has taken some drugs

C. He has taken a *lot* of drugs

B. He has taken a lot of drugs because back at Pyotr's apartment when a black tray, maybe a blue tray was handed to him, he didn't want anyone to know he was scared, okay, not scared, he'd just never done it before, never had the opportunity presented before

A. And so?

B. He did the lot!

A. For a moment Pyotr didn't say anything, he just looked at the young man like

C. "What the fuck did you just do?"

>(**A** *and* **C** *stare at* **B**. *An excruciating beat.*)

A. But then he laughed

And everyone laughed with him

A, B & C. HAHAHAHA

B. And nothing happened

Pyotr just came up to the young man as they were leaving and said

C. "I didn't think you were that kind of guy brother!

Where have you been all these years, I mean where have you been?"

B. And although the young man had never had a brother or even really a father or been very close to anyone and actually always thought of himself as the strong silent type, he remembered something he'd seen online about family being the people you surround yourself with and so said

"Where have I been?

Where have YOU been brother?

And yes, I love drugs, I do them all the time!"

> *(Beat.)*

C. And so

Now

A young man arrives at the front of the queue

B. Standing in front of the bouncer ready to /

A. "No"

B. "No?"

A. "No"

B. The bouncer laughs, shakes his head, and then looks at Pyotr, why the fuck is he looking at Pyotr, and says

A. "He's a child

And it's a school night"

> *(**B** is thrown off course.)*

C. Laughter ripples through the queue behind him

And he

A. What does he do then?

What does the young man do?

B. He straightens up

And says with the cold but kind of alluring anger that all great men in Russia have

"I'm not a child, I'm a fucking bank manager"

> *(They all roar in ecstasy. Nightclub music creeps in.)*

C. And they're in

B. Hands stamped

A. Bags checked

B. Shots poured

C. And he gathers them round

B. All these people the young man doesn't know but feels like he knows, feels like they know him

A. Raises his glass and says

B. "A toast!"

> *(Beat. We move to **C** as the sound of the nightclub becomes background music at the debt collector's party.)*

C. A debt collector watches his brother toast his health for the fifth fucking time and then stands and tells the table

"I'm going for a smoke

Finish your toast without me"

B. Takes the elevator

C. Fuck the stairs

A. And finds himself outside

In the warm still night.

> *(Beat. The storytellers exhale and settle for a moment before...)*

B. Someone leaving the building lets the door slam behind them

C. What is wrong with people?

A. But it's him

C. Not *him*

A. Winking and smiling and asking

C. But not ever *really* asking

B. "Brother

Heeeey little brother

Birthday boy

Can I bum one?

> (**C** *takes out a cigarette, his last, and reluctantly lights it for* **B**. *They stand in silence until...*)

How's work?"

A. Doesn't his brother know that all Russians hate small talk?

C. "Boring

You know how it is"

B. "Not really

My work is challenging but always exciting

But look

We both know there's worse things in life than a boring job

Most Russians could only dream of a boring job

Some monotony would do this nation good!"

A. A debt collector winces

C. But he gives his brother what he left all their adoring relatives to hear

"Thanks for the party

Really

I mean it"

B. "It was the least I could do little brother

They wanted to surprise you and Olga?

B. She begged me to help

But listen

I know things have been difficult the past few years

I know things have been difficult for everyone the past few years

But if you ever need money, what's a loan between brothers?"

C. And then he winks

Throws his cigarette in the grass by the door

And goes back to his party

B. A toast!

(Beat. We move to **A**, *an old woman.)*

A. An old woman stands in an apartment and makes cheese on toast

B. It is late

C. It is very late

A. But she can't sleep

You see her daughter was meant to call, said she would call

And nothing

No call

Her daughter asks her why she doesn't sleep

And her doctor tells her that this

Thing

Gets worse with no sleep

B & C. "Just sleep!"

A. They both say

B. "You've got all the time now to rest!"

C. "Why don't you try it?"

A. *Just*

Sleep

Just like that?

> (**A** *laughs.*)

Just call on bloody time

And so

Instead

An old woman makes her daughter cheese on toast

She is skating on the frozen court below their apartment

And like her mother used to say, "Hunger makes…"

"Hunger makes…"

C. "Hunger makes the cold grow worse"?

A. And look

Snow!

B. Where?

A. There!

> (**A** *points.*)

Falling like it used to

And so an old woman leaves the cheese on toast

C. She does?

A. Watch it, will you?

B. Er

A. And runs to the window to call her daughter inside

A. She think she's invincible but she's not, she's just young

Slides the window open and

> *(Beat.* **A** *stands, dumbfounded at the sight of...)*

No snow

No daughter

Just warm night air and the smell of burning

B & C. A toast!

> *(The storytellers begin to inhabit three respective spaces – a nightclub, courtyard and an apartment. As the scene builds, we don't always need to know whose thread is whose.)*

B. A young man sways through a club in Moscow, Russia

C. A debt collector stands and smokes

B. And he is proud

How could he not be proud?

It is literally fucking incredible

Bodies bathed in

A. Moonlight!

B. He didn't know silver light existed but there you go, we must have invented it

Girls

Candy floss

Girls eating candy floss

And a trampoline

A motherfucking trampoline!

C. A debt collector stands and smokes and remembers a party his mother threw him when he was eight

B. Everything is so beautiful

And big

Does it need to be that big?

No, but that's why it's perfect

C. They didn't have anything, nobody had anything

But she did it anyway

Asked everyone in their apartment to help

And at the end, after they had played games and sung songs, she brought out a bag of tangerines

She must have spent months tracking them down, how did she?

And then they sat in a circle and passed them round

A few segments each

But after it was all over

After everybody had gone home

He hid in the wardrobe holding the peel and cried

Cried she'd had to work so hard

Cried he'd had to share

Cried until his brother found him, sat him up and said

B. "Brother!

Hey little brother

Why do you always worry so much?

One day we'll both make a lot of money

And throw her a party with enough fruit for everyone

A tangerine each!"

(Beat.)

A. An old woman stands in front of an open window and realises it's not snowing, it was never snowing

Who said there was snow?

*(***B*** *laughs in amazement.)*

B. Bottles on ice and fire at the same time!

A. It must have been him

Does he think this is funny?

And so an old woman goes to the bedroom to tell him

"Stop laughing! Do you *want* cheese on toast?!"

B. And a young man turns round to share this with all the people he feels like he knows, feel like they know him

But they're gone

A. And she's shouting at an empty

A & B. Where has everyone gone?

B. And then a young man, realising he is alone, but also realising he's surrounded by people

Young, beautiful, proud to be *Russian* people

A. You get old and then everyone leaves you

B. Starts to dance.

(Beat. The music builds.)

C. A debt collector stands and

A. Smoke!

Is that

B. A smoke machine?

A. The campfire she built with her friends from the university

C. A debt collector stands and

A. Her mother burning chairs to keep them warm

B. Fuck yes it is!

A. Her first husband's cigarettes

Her second husband's factory clothes

Her third husband's Cuban cigars

He was disgusting, but he did make good meatballs

B. It's a motherfucking smoke machine!

A. And then the smell of smoke from a kitchen at the end of a hallway...

Her hallway

Her kitchen

Not then, now!

What's this?

Cheese on

B. A toast!

*(Beat. **B**'s dancing becomes bigger, wilder, faster.)*

C. And so

A debt collector bends slowly to pick up his brother's cigarette

Still wet and still warm

A. While

B. That old woman?

A. Opens every single window in an apartment in Moscow

C. And then he takes out his keys, finds the sharpest one with his thumb, walks up to the single shiny black car with the personalised number plate

C. The only new thing in the entire neighbourhood

And runs the key down the length of it

> *(The sound of metal on metal, not a million miles away from Russian nightclub music.)*

B. Sure she asked him the same questions

C. A line

B. But who cares?

C. Undeniable

B. Make your one day happen today

C. Unambiguous

B. TOO RIGHT!

> *(**B** goes out with a bang. The music stops.)*

C. And then a debt collector wipes a key on the side of his trousers

Nods at the not so fancy car now at home in his courtyard

And goes back inside to his party.

> *(**C** goes out with a quieter bang.)*

A. And an old woman eating burnt toast in a kitchen alone

Shivers

Puts her plate in the sink

And walks to her bedroom, her wardrobe

> *(Hearing this, **B** and **C** tentatively come back as storytellers in **A**'s story.)*

B. Her wardrobe?

A. Her daughter needs an extra coat and she knows

Like all good mothers in Moscow, Russia know

That you should always keep an extra coat for situations like

(**A** *feels something unexpected.*)

This

What's this?

Something smooth

Something wooden

Something rectangular

B & C. Something rectangular!

A. A box that Svetlana, her best friend who lives upstairs

(**B** *and* **C** *finally realise who Svetlana is.*)

B & C. Her best friend who lives upstairs!

A. Gave her

And then she lifts the box out and sits down very slowly because

Because

(*Beat.* **B** *and* **C** *wait for the penny to drop.*)

The box is full of money but she has no idea where it came from.

End of Act One

ACT TWO

Scene Eleven

The storytellers conjure up Sally, but there's a wild edge to her now.

B. A cat called Sally sees an opportunity and takes it

In the balcony room next to her balcony room, a window slides open

C. It is January

It is freezing

A. Well

We *are* in Moscow

Oh

We're still in Moscow by the way

B. Yes

We're still in Moscow

And it is six months later

And the rumours are true

It *is* cold

C. But

The flats are communally heated

Yes the flats are *still* uncomfortably, unbearably overheated

A. And so Sally knows

C. Like all cats across Moscow know

A. That as the sun goes down, windows slide open.

> *(Beat.)*

B. Sally hears the click and jumps up

A. These days?

No time to waste

C. Balances on the sill and tries not to look down

B. Five floors below

Cars

Tarmac

And a courtyard covered in snow

C. What cars?

What tarmac?

A. Sally doesn't look down remember!

Out of sight, out of mind

C. And then she jumps

B. A figure suspended in the night air

> *(They hold their breath.)*

A & C. And she makes it!

> *(They celebrate.)*

B. Of course she makes it

She may be eighteen nearly nineteen years old but she's lived through a lot

And *this*

Is important.

(Beat.)

C. Sally jumps down into the balcony room next door where

B. Pickles pickling

Underwear drying

And a cat called Vanessa

A. The Russian blue who's been sharing her food with Sally for months

C. "Quick, eat"

B. Says Vanessa

C. "*Sherlock Holmes* special is on in a minute"

A. Sally doesn't need to be told anymore

Doesn't need to be given reminders of when it's dinner time anymore

She eats because she's hungry

B. She eats because she is really hungry

A. She's still a cat

She's still Sally

C. But something's changed, you know?

(Beat.)

A. Once she's finished, Vanessa doesn't leave as usual

But instead says

C. "I've been asked to remind you that everything you've been eating since she stopped feeding you, you've got to give back

In some way or another"

B. "But it's Christmas Eve

There's too much to go around anyway!"

A. Vanessa's eyes narrow

C. "Look

We all know you're in a difficult situation

And we feel for you, we really do, but

We're not a charity

And even if we were

You're not the kind of cat that takes charity, are you?"

B. Sally's tail flicks

A & B. Dammit

C. But she does the smart thing and says

A. "I'll remember

See you tomorrow"

B. And then

Not knowing when the old woman will decide to start feeding her again

A. Not knowing whether the old woman will ever decide to start feeding her again

C. Not knowing whether she'll even be able to pay Vanessa back if the old woman does start feeding her again

Sally jumps back

A. Elegant once more in the night air

(They all hold their breath.)

C. Except that at that precise moment

Just as she's about to reach her balcony room window and make this

A. Perfect

B. And precise

A. Landing

C. She realises that the window has been shut

A. Wait

B. What?

C. And without having time to wonder

B. Why or when or who

A. Or get angry about the colossal fuck up that happened somewhere between now and ten minutes ago

C. She falls five floors down

To the cars and the tarmac and the courtyard covered in snow.

(They sing a verse of a Russian Orthodox chant. It is all very sad and very dramatic.)

Scene Twelve

An unexpected holy moment.

C. A debt collector stands in a church in Moscow, Russia.

> *(Beat. **A** and **B** were not expecting this to be
> the case.)*

A. Oh

Does he?

C. Well it's Christmas Eve, isn't it?

B. *Russian* Christmas Eve

January sixth

Some parties, some fireworks

But no one at church except for

C. True believers.

> *(Beat.)*

And so a debt collector stands in a church and looks up
at the ceiling, magnificent above him

Hands on hearts in a sea of blue

And gold

B. So *much* gold

A. Freshly painted

C. Russia can't build churches fast enough

Did you know Russia can't build churches fast enough?

Every day, three new ones appear across this holy land

A. And last year

B. Our beloved 2018

C. Twenty-five appeared in Moscow alone

A, B & C. Amen.

>   *(Beat. They cross themselves.)*

B. But not everyone's happy

A. "Build schools"

B. "Hospitals"

A. "We don't want more churches

>   We don't need more churches"

B. "Look at us

>   Outside
>
>   Protesting!"

C. Bullshit

>   He hasn't seen a protest
>
>   Have *you* seen a protest?

>>   *(They're silent.)*

>   No
>
>   Because a church is all of those things too
>
>   In its own way

A, B & C. Amen.

>   *(Beat. They cross themselves.)*

C. You see

>   A debt collector stands in a church because his mother cannot

A. She's not dead

C. No one said she was dead!

B. But two strokes down

Bed-bound and quiet

A. Cared for most days by his wife Olga, who's had to quit her job to help out

C. And as he feels the space where his mother usually stands grow emptier, darker, quieter

Has there ever been a more important time to come

Be here?

>*(Beat.)*

You see

A debt collector lights a candle

A, B & C. Amen

>*(They cross themselves.)*

C. Because medicine is expensive

A. It's true

B. Do you know how expensive medicine in Russia is?

C. Because even if you do your homework

Even if you know the pharmacist

Even if you take on more clients, more debt, more being shouted at like a dog

A. More standing

At church

Praying

C. It's still only your brother who can afford to step in, afford to be told that

A. "Thank God you're around"

B. "Yes thank God you're around"

A, B & C. Amen

> (**A** *and* **B** *cross themselves –* **C** *doesn't.*)

A. "So amazing you helped"

B. "With the year that you've had"

A. "And the car"

B. *"And the car"*

A. "Nasty but not surprising

Bandits on the streets"

B. "Cost a fortune to fix and you still covered her bills"

A. "Still found time to check in"

B. "We are forever in your debt"

A. "Forever in your debt"

B. "Forever and ever in your /"

C. "ENOUGH! /"

B. "Debt".

> (*Awkward beat. Someone clears their throat.*)

C. And so a debt collector stands in a church in Moscow, Russia because his mother is ill and medicine is expensive and his brother is an asshole and this

Place

This beautiful sacred don't you dare question it *Russian* place

Is the *only* place that makes sense

The *only* place that gives him strength to do

What he needs to do.

> (**C** *prays.*)

C. "Wash me thoroughly from mine iniquity, and cleanse me from my sin

Sprinkle me with hyssop, and I shall be made whiter than snow

Create in me a clean heart, and renew a right spirit within me

Let me teach transgressors Thy ways, so that the ungodly shall turn back unto thee."

*(**A** and **B** wrap up – a little unnerved.)*

B. And then a debt collector leaves a church in Moscow, Russia

A. And walks his family three blocks to the courtyard where they live.

C. And then he says

"I won't be long

Back in time for dinner

They just need me to check the CCTV"

A. Wait

Sorry

I thought he was in a church in Moscow, Russia?

C. He was

B. I thought it was Christmas Eve?

C. Exactly

And so a debt collector knows, like all debt collectors who are good at their job know

That the ones who aren't usually in

Will be.

Scene Thirteen

> *Total confusion.*

B. A phone rings in an apartment

C. A phone rings in an apartment on the fifth floor of an apartment block

B. A phone rings in an apartment on the fifth floor of an apartment block in Moscow, Russia.

> *(Beat. **B** and **C** look at **A** – is she going to pick up the phone?)*

C. A phone rings in an apartment

B. A phone rings in an apartment on the fifth floor of an apartment block

C. A phone rings in an apartment on the fifth floor of an apartment block in Moscow, Russia.

> *(Beat. Still nothing.)*

B. A phone rings in an apartment on the fifth floor of an apartment block in Moscow, Russia and an old woman thinks after quite a bit of ringing

C. After quite a *lot* of ringing

B. This is getting even more repetitive than it was before!

C. Goes to the phone and /

A. No

A phone rings in an apartment but an old woman just lets it

You see

An old woman actually has things to do

B. On Christmas Eve?

A. Like locking the doors

C. Are they not locked already?

A. Like *checking* she's locked the doors

If you didn't need all these doors then why would they make the whole thing so complicated in the first place?

And then

C. A phone rings in an apartment on the fifth floor of an apartment block?

A. An old woman turns on the TV

(Mock talk show voices.)

B. "Do you know what they're playing over there?"

C. "Go on, surprise me!"

B. "A dangerous" /

C. "Oh yes, we all know this"

B & C. "A DANGEROUS GAME!"

C. Turns it up loud enough to drown out the ringing

A. And then she goes to check on the balcony room

You see they come through the windows now

I mean you've never been safe

In an apartment

In Russia

But at least they used to knock on the door and give you some warning!

(Beat. **B** *and* **C** *realise what's happened.)*

B. Wait

C. So she's the one who shut the window on Sally?

A. This has got nothing to do with Sally

If windows are open, an old woman shuts them

We need to move on.

> *(Beat. The ringing, and **A**'s lack of interest in it, is starting to get to **B** and **C**.)*

C. Okay so, a phone rings in an apartment

A. She knows!

B. She does?

C. Does she really?

A. She's just

This is all just

Look.

> *(Beat.)*

An old woman lets a phone ring because at some point

Somewhere in between you all leaving and you all coming back

She didn't

Put down her tea and ran to it thinking

Someone is calling, someone never calls

Daughter

Doctor

Friend?

She's lost track of who is dead and alive but it *could* be a friend

C. An alive friend

A. And although shortly after hanging up, she forgot what the man on the phone had said, who he was and why he had called

A. He rang the next day while she was in the bath

B. And the following day while she was making meatballs

C. And the day after that while she was reading the paper

B. Writing a letter?

C. Feeding Sally dinner?

A. Until she knew that if someone called, that if *anyone* called, it was to say something bad

B. Something like?

C. "You owe money and you need to pay it back

You owe money and you need to pay it back or bad things are going to happen"

A. Yes!

That's the one.

> *(Beat.)*

And so an old woman lets a phone ring because she knows that it isn't safe to pick up anymore

B. Take a bath anymore

C. Make meatballs

B. Feed Sally

C. Go out

B. See friends

A. And so she focuses on the things that she can control

Like the windows

Like the doors

The only things that will ensure that whatever

C. "Bad things are going to happen"

A. Don't.

(Beat.)

B. Okay but

Isn't it Christmas Eve?

A. Is it?

C. January sixth, remember

B. And so although phones are ringing for bad reasons

They're also ringing for good reasons

And an old woman letting a phone ring and ring and

C. Yep, still ringing

B. Doesn't know

Can't know if /

A. It's him!

B. OR if it's someone calling to wish her a Merry Christmas

If it's someone calling to check up on her

If

Actually

It's her daughter.

(Beat.)

A. Hm

Have *you* heard from her daughter?

And have *you* heard from her daughter?

And has anyone seen her daughter step foot in this apartment through any of this?

(They have not.)

So while an old woman would love to believe that it's Christmas Eve

A. Would love to believe that her daughter is calling to check up on her

Say something

Say anything

She's run to the phone enough times to know that it's not.

    (Beat.)

C. A neighbour bangs on the door and shouts

B. "What's going on?

Turn the damn TV down!"

A. And an old woman /

See!

First they call, then they bang on the door

Isn't it a good thing she locked it?

Goes to check on the money

B. She remembers the money now?

C. The money her daughter sent or the money she /

A. An old woman doesn't remember when or how or why she got the money

You'd never get anything done if you had to explain how things worked round here

All she knows is that sometime between the ringing and the running and the running and the ringing and the calls telling her

C. "You owe money and you need to pay it back"

A. She knew that keeping it all in one place was a very bad idea.

    (Beat.)

B. And so now?

A. It's everywhere!

And so she starts by checking the sugar pot

B. Money's there

A. Cat food dispenser

C. There

A. Little nook beside the radiator

C. Also there

A. Behind the framed photo of her father in military uniform

B. Money!

Lots of it

A. Laundry basket

C. Yes

A. Plastic box with all her sachets of mayonnaise

B. Yes

A. How many was that?

B. Six no

Seven

Six?

A. Better go back

(Lightning speed.)

Plastic box

B. Yes

A. Radiator

C. Yes

A. Laundry basket

B. Yep

A. Photo

C. Yes

A. Did we do radiator?

C. Sure

B. Does an old woman write a list of these places?

C. Yes, an old woman writes a list of these places!

A. No

If there's anything her second husband taught her before he was taken away it was that if you need to hide your money, no, *when* you need to hide your money

The stupidest thing you could do is write down a list

And so now, she is done

Money

Windows

Money

Done

And once she's finally had a minute to sit down and decide what to do with her morning

B. She remembers one last thing

C. Time to feed Sally!

A. Why wouldn't she remember that?

And so she fills Sally's bowl, hits it three times like she does everyday, and waits.

(Beat. Sally doesn't come.)

She'll be here any minute.

(Beat. Sally still doesn't come.)

B. An old woman stands in a kitchen on the fifth floor of an apartment block and

C. A phone that has been ringing for the last half hour

Stops

(A sigh of relief.)

A. But an old woman doesn't notice

B. An old woman doesn't notice because the television is turned up too loud?

C. An old woman doesn't notice because she's become oblivious to the ringing?

A. No

An old woman doesn't notice because she realises with a rare but undeniable clarity that something else has happened

Something else really bad has happened

Sally is missing.

Scene Fourteen

A wild carousel.

C. A debt collector presses a buzzer

B. A cat wakes up

A. An old woman leaves an apartment

B. A cat wakes up

C. A debt collector /

(A sharp inhale.)

B. A cat wakes up in a courtyard in Moscow, Russia

Yeah

She knows what you're thinking

Sally thought it too

Eighteen years of sofas and sitcoms flashed before her eyes

The feeling you get when you watch the person you love open a can of tuna with your name on it

Gone

Forever

But Sally's a cat, remember?

And in a city of apartments and communal heating, this actually happens a lot

A & C. "Raining cats"

B. They call it.

*(Beat. We move to **A**, an old woman.)*

A. An old woman leaves an apartment

An old woman leaves an apartment on the fifth floor of an apartment block

An old woman leaves an apartment on the fifth floor of an apartment block because her cat is missing and she knows

Like all old women across Moscow, Russia know

That if this happens after being told

C. "Bad things are going to happen"

A. That she has no choice but to take matters into her own hands

And so she packs three photos of Sally

A handful of rubles

And a small sharp knife

Who knows who she's going to run into?

And then an old woman leaves an /

B. Wait

Has she not left yet?

I thought she was leaving

A. She *is* leaving

She's just

An old woman hasn't left her apartment in months, okay?

(**A** *does the following in real time.*)

Hasn't put on her shoes

Combed her hair

Turned the locks left instead of right

Stood in the stairway with the draft around her ankles, the elevator ringing in her bones, and the silence all around her.

(Beat. We move to **C**, *a debt collector.)*

C. A debt collector presses a buzzer in the lobby of an apartment block

B. "What do you want!?"

A. Shouts a voice down the intercom

C. And so he tells this kid for the fifth maybe sixth time this month

"You owe money and you need to pay it back

You owe money and /"

B. "It's Christmas Eve you sicko!

Have some respect

I know my rights"

A. And then the line goes dead

B. But a debt collector doesn't leave

C. No

A debt collector presses the buzzer

A debt collector presses the same buzzer in the same apartment block so that the kid knows he signed whatever rights he had away when he made his first bad decision

(Buzz.)

His second bad decision

(Buzz.)

His third bad decision

(Continuous buzzing.)

This is Russia you little shit

And there are no free lunches in Russia!

(The buzzer breaks.)

And then he lights a cigarette, takes a few long drags

And drops it into the idiot kid's letterbox

Oops.

*(Beat. We move to **B**, a cat called Sally.)*

B. A cat called Sally wakes up in a courtyard and realises that she is alive

Realises that she has landed in a pile of snow

And then realises that her tail is broken

Shit

You hear about it but you don't really believe it until it happens to you

Sally needs to get home

Fast.

(Beat.)

But hey

The good news is that cats have an excellent sense of direction

Sally watched a program about it on Animal Planet *just* yesterday

Thought

If I were ever in a situation where I needed to find my way home

I'd be fine

Right?

*(Beat. We move to **A**, an old woman.)*

A. An old woman knocks on a door on the sixth floor of an apartment block because it's her friend Svetlana's door and she /

C. "Yes?!"

A. Says a woman with a drink in one hand and a man in the other

As if she's interrupted an event reserved for incredibly important young people

"I'm looking for Svetlana"

C. "You are?"

A. "I am"

C. "Right

Now?"

A. "Right now"

The woman gives her a look

The kind of look incredibly important young people give her

But returns with another young woman who says

B. "Can I help?"

A. "I'm looking for Svetlana"

*(**B** and **C** giggle hysterically.)*

B & C. "We know!"

B. "I *am* Svetlana"

C. "She *is* Svetlana"

A. "No

Svetlana who lives here

Who comes round for tea

Who'd know what to /"

B. "We're only in Moscow for the holidays"

C. "We heard the Christmas lights here are the best in the world"

B. "Do you want us to call the guy we're renting from?"

(*Beat. We move to* **C**, *a debt collector.*)

C. A debt collector knocks on a door on the ground floor of an apartment block

A. "Can I help?"

B. Asks a woman with tinsel in her hair and a baby on her hip

C. "You owe money and you need to pay it back

You owe money and you need to pay it back or bad things are going to happen"

B. Her face changes

From polite to confused to upset then to angry

A. And she slams the door!

C. But he puts his foot in

A. She struggles

C. He adds some pressure

A. She cries out

C. Does she think he's never dealt with a slamming door before?

B. And wait!

The baby slips

A. The baby slips?!

C. But he catches it, steps back and says

"I'll look after it

And you can go get the money".

*(Beat. We move to **B**, a cat called Sally.)*

B. A cat

Er

A cat called

Sorry

A cat called Sally gets her bearings in a courtyard in

Block A, block B, block C, block

Shit!

This is what happens when all the buildings look the same!

Because as Sally tries to figure out where she is

Place the things she knows

So well

She realises you can spend your whole life looking at something

A place you thought you knew

And then you fall five floors from an apartment window and realise you didn't know it

Not really

And however incredible your night vision, sense of direction, personality, looks

If you don't know what to do when shit hits the fan then you are well and truly /

*(Beat. We move to **A**, an old woman.)*

A. An old woman knocks on a door on the seventh floor of an apartment block and /

*(**B** raises his hand to silence her.)*

B. No need

A man eating a pastry answers

A. And so an old woman holds up a picture of Sally and explains the situation

And he listens

Just like they used to

And then when she's finished

B. And then when *he's* finished

Damn that was tasty!

A. He tilts his head to one side and says

B. "I'd love to help, I really would but

That's not a picture of a cat

That's a knife

Are you sure your cat is missing?

Are you sure you even have a cat?"

(Beat. We move to **C**, *a debt collector.)*

C. And so a debt collector arrives /

B. And so a cat called Sally despairs

C. And so /

A. An old woman walks up to the eighth and final floor

C. No

No

And so a debt collector arrives at the building of his third and final client of the evening

An old woman who lives in one of those really fucking nice buildings in Kutuzovsky

Okay?!

*(***C*** *raises his finger to buzz.)*

B. Wait!

C. What?!

B. On Christmas Eve?

A. Really?

C. She's been messing him around for months

At first he thought she'd be easy

Called, explained the usual

A. And she was scared

B. She *was* really scared

C. A little bit of being scared can be healthy

But then, nothing happened

No transfer

No commission

And when he called the next day and the next day and the next

She'd always say something different, like

A. "Svetlana, is that you again?"

C. Or

A. "Sally needs meatballs"

C. Or

A. "How dare you call me directly and who gave you my name?"

C. Like she was playing a game

Winding him up and succeeding!

And then she stopped answering altogether

And so

Although it's Christmas Eve

And although his family is at home waiting

Who else is going to do the right thing?

You take money, you pay it back

There are no free lunches in Russia!

*(Beat. **C** realises he's shouting.)*

He'll have a cigarette first.

*(Beat. We move to **A**, an old woman.)*

A. An old woman arrives on the eighth floor and finds Tanya

Cured meat Tanya

Waiting for the elevator to arrive

B. "You're on the wrong floor!

Number's on the key, remember?"

A. And an old woman thinks

I know, you moron

I've lived here since before your father was born!

But she doesn't say this

She never says what she thinks anymore, does she?

She just tells Tanya that

"I know this isn't my floor but thank you for the reminder

I'm here because I'm looking for

I'm looking for"

*(**A** trails off, unable to remember Sally's name.)*

B. Cured meat Tanya raises her eyebrows and punches the elevator button again

A. This is ridiculous, Tanya knows who she means!

B. "Better take the stairs or I'm going to miss all the fun

It'll be morning before that old thing comes up!"

A. "Sally, you idiot

She's looking for Sally!"

B. But Tanya's gone, too far down now to hear her

A. Silence

The draft around her ankles

Elevator ringing in her bones

Louder

Louder

B & C. Ding!

A. And then it opens

Right there

As if it's come all the way up just for her.

> *(A steps into the elevator as we move to* **C***, a debt collector, standing outside the building.)*

C. A debt collector buries his cigarette in the snow and presses the buzzer

> *(No response.)*

Presses again

> *(Still no response.)*

Presses a third time when /

B. The door opens and a woman with a smoky smell steps outside

C. Not cigarettes but

Meat?

B. "Waiting for someone?"

C. "279"

The woman with the meaty smell rolls her eyes and laughs

B. "She's looking for you

Here!"

C. And then she opens the door

People never open the door for him

B. "Have a good night!"

C. And he's in

Silence

The draft around his ankles

The elevator buzzing as it gets

A. Louder

B. Louder

A & B. Di /

C. But just as it arrives he thinks

Better take the stairs

He's not doing anything wrong but just

Better take the stairs.

    (Beat.)

A. An old woman steps outside of an apartment block

B. A cat called Sally tries to stay calm

A. And realises it is dark

B. When did it get so dark?

A. Realises it is cold

B. When did it get so cold?

A. Wraps her dressing gown around her and realises

They don't make winter coats like they used to

A & B. And then she realises that the courtyard is filling with people

A. Maybe one of them will help!

B. That's never a good sign

C. A debt collector arrives at the old woman's apartment

Puts an ear to the door

TV's on

An eye to the spy hole

Lights are all on

A. And so an old woman walks out across the courtyard when

B. Sally sees her

C. A debt collector rings the bell

B. Sally sees *her*

A. People start shouting

C. And again and again and

Fuck!

He shouldn't be here

He should be at home with his family!

A. They must have seen Sally

C. She must be in

B. Wait

Stop!

C. Rings

A. And so an old woman runs over snow, over ice

B. And Sally

Despite her fall, despite her tail

A. And her knees

B. And *her* knees

Runs

C. *Rings*

B. No

Runs!

Towards an old woman

Her old woman

Her less than perfect but still her old woman

When

Just as they're about to make a perfect and precise reunion

She realises why they're shouting

A. Did they find her?

B. Fireworks

A. Is she safe?

B. Ruuuuuuuuun /

> *(A loud bang and a flash of gold. **A** is transported somewhere else.)*

A. A sunset on the Volga

Her first time inside the Bolshoi theatre

A. His car backfiring as they drove across the Urals

Her cooker

Finally breaking.

> *(Beat.)*

An old woman rides an elevator back up to the fifth floor of an apartment block in Moscow, Russia

B. No Sally?

A. No Sally

Just the draft around her ankles, the ringing in her bones and the

> *(Something different.)*

And then as she exits the elevator and takes down the key from round her neck

She realises with a rare but undeniable certainty that something is different

Something is most certainly

Cigarettes?

The smell of someone who smokes a lot of cigarettes

C. And then a debt collector spins around and sees an old woman holding a key that says "Apartment 279".

Scene Fifteen

A total, utter nightmare.

B. A cat called Sally sits at the side of a road in Moscow, Russia

    (**A** *and* **C** *celebrate.*)

A. She most certainly does!

C. Talk about nine lives /

B. Don't

    It isn't over yet

    Because a cat called Sally sits at the side of *a road in Moscow, Russia*

    THERE'S A REASON CATS DON'T LEAVE THE COURTYARDS HERE!

    (*Beat. It's true.*)

C. Cars speed past five lanes deep

A. On *each* side

B. Sally had seen the reports on TV

C. "Worst traffic in the world

    And the pollution

    Also the worst in the world"

B. But they'd always ended on a positive note with news about

A. "Pedestrianised areas, electric buses with free wifi, bike lanes, bike bells and traffic lights"

B. Sally can't see a traffic light anywhere!

    (*Beat.*)

C. A carton, thrown from a car speeding past, hits Sally

A, B & C. Jesus!

B. And she collides with two Chihuahuas walking a man down the road

A. "A cat like you doesn't wanna be out here!"

B. They snap

C. "Not on Christmas Eve!"

A & C. "Go home!"

B. As if she wasn't trying already!

I mean

Sally sits at the side of the road because Sally is unable to return to the courtyard for fear of

C. Certain death

B. And unable to cross the road for fear of

C. Also certain death

A. She just needs a trustworthy human to pick her up and take her home.

(Beat. They look.)

B. What about them?

A. Nope

B. Him?

C. Does he look like a cat person?

A. And then they see her

A, B & C. Yes!

A. A woman wearing a big fluffy jumper covered in

C. Cats

Tabby cats

Lots and lots of tabby cats

B. The woman runs down some steps

C. Where is she going?

A. Who cares?

If tabby woman runs down some steps, so does Sally!

One

B. But she is quick

A. Two

B. And Sally is old

A. Three!

B. And as soon as she appeared, she's gone

Fading into the darkness in front of them.

(Beat. Eerie stillness.)

C. What *is* this place?

B. Sally's not so sure

Not so sure at all

A. There are shops selling trinkets and kiosks selling pastries

B. Sally would kill for a pastry but every cat knows they taste like shit from the kiosks

A. And it's full of people behaving very strangely

Not looking at Sally

Not looking at each other

B. Just staring straight ahead in the direction they're walking

C. But *where* are they walking?

(A traditional Russian tune begins to play softly.)

A. They're walking towards the music

B. And so Sally walks towards the music

C. Music is a good sign!

A. It's coming from a man in a red suit with a white fluffy beard and

Wait

B. Is that?

C. No

B. Is that really?

A, B & C. Father Frost!

(Beat.)

B. And so Sally just

C. Stops to enjoy the music

A. Thinks

B. Maybe there are *some* ups to this crazy city

C. Wonders

A. Is he going to take me home in his sleigh or via another means of transport?

(They exhale happily.)

C. When at that precise moment

A. That precise moment?

B. What now?

C. Father Frost grabs her!

A. Father Frost?

Are you sure?

C. Hoists her high above his head

B. Put her down

Put her down!

C. Booms

"Look boys and girls, it's Matroskin!"

B. What is he talking about?!

C. "Come see Matroskin dance!"

A. I'm Sally!

B. And she realises his beard isn't even real

A. And that the music isn't even live, it's actually coming from a speaker

C. "Gather round, there you go!"

A. And that sometimes in life you don't have time to plan or worry about what happens next

B. Digs her claws deep into his fingers

A. Deliver presents with those, you stupid fuck!

B. And runs back down the tunnel and up to the street.

(The music builds into something bigger, wilder.)

A. Except

B. Oh no

C. Shit

A. Oh Jesus, no

B. It's the other side of the road!

A. More people

B. More cars

C. More everything!

B. The broom of a street sweeper catches up with her

A. "What's a cat doing here?"

C. And she collides with a chain of children bundled up in winter onesies

B. One child grabs her

A. Another child screams

A & B. "AAAAAAAAAAAH!"

C. Two policeman holding guns decorated with tinsel look her way

A. Maybe they can help an eighteen nearly nineteen year old tabby?

B. Don't be naive

She's got to get back to the other side of the road!

C. But all Sally can focus on right now is not getting trampled by

B. A woman selling plastic flowers

C. A man holding a Bible

A. A German Shepherd

B. "You lost, love?"

A. Is that another Father Frost?

B. And then she sees it

The only building on the entire street that looks inviting or safe!

A. There's a picture on the front of a man, who looks friendly and is

B. Smiling

Look!

He's smiling

C. And so although Sally doesn't know what the sign says or even means, she knows, she just *knows* by some divine feline intuition that

A, B & C. This

Is the place.

(Beat. Disconcerting familiarity.)

A. A cat walks into a bank and is surprised by just how calm everything is

B. How quiet and still, no traffic, no voices

C. A different world

A. Carpet spins out for what seems like an eternity and while this would normally excite Sally, offer up endless opportunities for Sally

C. I mean, carpet!

A. It makes her head hurt and her tail spin

B. Men and women nod in appreciation

C. Weird

A. And other men and women talk quietly behind screens

B. Okay...

A. And whether it's the knowledge that when humans talk quietly it means trouble or the

C. Smell of bleach

B. Radiators on full blast

C. Her fall

A. The fireworks

B. The last six minutes no six hours no six MONTHS that have been just a bit too much for an eighteen nearly nineteen year old tabby to handle

A. Sally collapses

In a bank in Moscow, Russia.

Scene Sixteen

> **B** *smiles. Finally, his turn.*

B. A young man walks up to a cat

A young man walks up to a cat that has just walked into a bank

A young man

At first he can't believe it

A cat in a bank!?

But if there's anything that the last six months have taught him it's to expect the unexpected

What's that saying?

"When a man is tired of Moscow, he's tired of life!"

> *(Beat.)*

A young man walks up to a /

A. Sorry

I don't

C. *We* don't

A. The young man sold the loan

Set things in motion

But we're onto bigger, more important things now

The fireworks?

The phone calls?

B. But we're in *his* bank

C. Are you sure?

B. Yes!

A. Okay but does he still even work here?

B. Of course he still works here!

And *you* might be done with the young man

And *you* might be done with him

But the thing is

Are they?

Because that's all good and what did you say, "important"

But his story isn't over

You see

Ever since that crazy fateful too good to be true day when his manager invited him to rise to the challenge

When the buzz of the world cup still lingered in the air

A. When an old woman walked into a bank?

B. Exactly

A. I'm not finished

B. Ever since then he has been on a journey!

You want some character development?

COME ON!

(**B** *begins doing push ups.*)

I mean he works out now

Starts each day with thirty minutes at the outdoor gym in his apartment complex now

It hurt at first

A. It really did

B. But what do you do if something hurts?

You wrestle it to the ground!

(This could involve an audience member.)

Those long boring Metro journeys?

Only the boring get bored!

He uses them now

Milks each moment of them now

Reads books

C. Classic Russian books

B. Do you know how classic our classic Russian books are?

A. Memorises inspirational quotes

B. "The only regret you'll ever have is the chances you didn't take!"

C. Practises his Mandarin

B. "Yīgè niánqīng rén xiànzài shuō pǔtōnghuà"

(An awkward beat.)

That's a young man speaks Mandarin *in* Mandarin!

And he figures out whose party he's been invited to that evening

A commute is a great time to organise what we can now all agree is

A pretty busy social life!

And then he arrives at the bank

Bumps fists with the guy sweeping the pavement outside the doors

Walks past the queue of pensioners waiting to see him

And calls everyone into his office to talk about today's new initiative

Because yes

B. It *is* the same bank and *yes* he still works there

But

Well

Same same but different because the biggest change yes the biggest change of all is that he has recently been promoted to

THE BRANCH MANAGER

Or as he likes to paraphrase

Manager to the other bank managers.

>   *(Beat.)*

A & C. "That's not your job title!"

B. His employees love to joke

But you know what, in a position of power, you can't please everyone

Someone *will* say

A. "How did this happen?"

B. Or

C. "Does he deserve it?"

B. Or

A. "The Employee of the Month board is getting kind of boring"

>   *(**B** recreates his Employee of the Month photograph.)*

Wait

B. And so a young man walks up to a cat that has just walked into a bank because as branch manager

Any*one* or any

Cat

That comes through those doors is an opportunity

The beginning of a valued customer relationship.

    (Beat. **A** *and* **C** *look at* **B***, waiting.)*

C. "Oh for God's sake, I'll take care of it"

B. Says Dima or Grisha or whatever the security guard who always complains is called

C. "It's just a stray"

B. But a young man

Wait!

A young man's filling them in

It's been a while, hasn't it?

A. Well go on then

B. A young man strides up to the cat, scoops her up in one strong movement and says

"She's not a stray

She has a collar and she lives just across the road! She's probably lost

Her owner's probably worried sick

I'll take her back".

    (Beat.)

A. The customers waiting to be seen before the bank closes for the holidays in

C. Thirty bloody minutes!

B. Clap

And cheer

And a young man jumps onto a chair, cat safe in his newly toned arms and says

B. "Everyone inside this building will be seen before closing

Doesn't matter if we have to run over

Because it is 2019

And we are in Russia goddammit!"

A. "But why do *you* get to go home?"

B. One of his employees say as if they don't remember that it's Christmas Eve

A. Well no, exactly

B. Exactly!

Russian Christmas Eve

Like Christmas Eve but

Better

And for the first time in a very long time it actually means something because a young man is hosting his very first

RUSSIAN CHRISTMAS PARTAAAAAAY!

> (**B** *runs around, conjuring an imaginary apartment, imaginary music, imaginary guests.*)

Champagne

Caviar

Balloons

Caviar

You name it he's bought it

Curated a playlist

A guest list

Few of his mother's friends

Few of his

Cousins

Neighbours

Fun ones they have a pre-existing relationship with

And

Even his dad is on a flight over

And don't forget how expensive travel is during the holiday season.

*(**A** and **C** are impressed.)*

For the first time it's not a holiday to sit in the corner to

Grit your teeth to get through

It's a celebration of them and of him and of him treating them and so

Yeah

A young man walks up to a cat because of all these things, because of all of them but also because

At a party you want to have something called a party piece

Like a story that you and only you can tell

And this?

This is going to be a good one.

*(Beat. We move to **A** and **C**, a cat called Sally.)*

A. A cat called Sally lets herself be carried back to an apartment in Moscow, Russia

C. She's fine by the way

Just needed some milk

A. Passes the crowds by the Metro

C. Is that where she was?

A. Passes Father Creeping Frost in the underpass

C. Pervert

A. And arrives back up to her side of the road

C. Well of course it makes sense from up here!

A. A crowd leaves her courtyard while policemen with sparkly guns push a boy into a van

C. "It was just fireworks!"

He's saying

A. Just fireworks

Just fireworks?

Lock him up

C. And throw away the key.

      *(Beat. We move to **B**, a young man.)*

B. A young man arrives at an apartment block in Moscow, Russia

He passes it on his way to work but up close it's even nicer

The owner's probably put out a reward that's been accumulating for weeks

Or maybe there's no reward BUT upon recognising the selflessness with which he's taken time out of his *Christmas Eve* party of the year day

They'll offer him money

He'll say

"No need

I'm making pretty sweet dosh now"

But when they insist he'll do the right thing and say "Okay".

> *(Beat. We move to **A** and **C**, a cat called Sally.)*

A. A cat called Sally watches the boy punch the buzzer on the wall over and over again

C. What does he think that's going to achieve?

She disconnected it weeks ago

A. And Sally she does what she always does

Waits for the human to realise the obvious.

> *(Beat. We move to **B**, a young man.)*

B. A young man realises he needs to think outside the buzz and tries the next buzzer up

C. "Helloooooo?"

A. Shouts a voice down the intercom

B. "I'm looking for apartment 279?"

C. "No can do

We're in the eighties, baby!"

B. "No

Wait!

I have their cat

279's cat

It's kind of funny actually

She walked into my bank

A cat in a bank!"

> *(Beat.)*

For a moment there's silence and a young man thinks

B. Did they not hear the joke?

But then they laugh and say

C. "Come on up

Svetlana will love this."

*(Beat. We move to **A** and **C**, a cat called Sally.)*

A. A cat called Sally rides the elevator up to the fifth floor of her apartment block

C. She's heard it but she's never ridden it, you know?

A. And she does have to admit that it's actually pretty cool

C. But Sally does wish the boy from the bank would put her down

A. He's holding her tight

And Sally knows

C. Like all cats her age know

A. That this kind of embrace?

It isn't for her

C. It's for him.

*(Beat. We move to **B**, a young man.)*

B. A young man arrives to the fifth floor of an apartment block

It's a bit of a mess, not how he keeps his own landing but he's not here to judge

Picks up a dead plant lying on its side by the door

There's no such thing as being too helpful

Wipes his shoes on the mat

It's the right thing to do

And then rings the bell and waits.

(Beat.)

For a long time nothing happens and a young man thinks

They're not in

After all that they're not even in

C. But then he hears someone shuffling

Presses his ear to the leather

Calls

B. "Excuse me, 279?

I've got your cat

Sorry but I've got your cat

Thanks!"

C. For a moment the shuffling stops

B. But then it grows louder

C. Closer

B. And a young man steps back, straightens up, runs a hand through his hair ready to give the cat back, claim his reward and

> *(A light flicks on revealing **A**. **B** is stunned, baffled by the turn the story has taken.)*

Who?

C. The woman

The old woman

The old woman who walked into the bank that day

That good day

Remember?

B. He's had lots of good days

C. Well he has now

But back then, they were few and far between

She was his first

B. He doesn't like to dwell on the past

Don't you know that most great men in Russia don't like to dwell on the past?

(Beat.)

And is it her?

I mean she looks

C. Older, paler, thinner

B. Mind plays tricks and so

A young man hands *an* old woman a cat

C. All the while avoiding her eyes

B. Turns around

Where were the stairs?

A. But just as he's doing this, just as he's about to walk away

B. And get to his party, can we just get to his party?

A. An old woman walks up, touches him on the shoulder and says

"Well aren't you going to come inside then?"

B. "Why?"

A. "You brought back Sally, didn't you?

I can't let you go without thanking you"

B. And so a young man

A young man...

C. Goes inside

What's the problem?

B. Well

C. Is something wrong?

  (Beat.)

B. No!

Why would anything be wrong?

No, a young man follows an old woman who may or may not have been his client, who knows, not important, but who is the old woman whose cat he brought back, saved, wants to thank him, of course wants to thank him, briefly, okay, through the door, through the hallway, into the kitchen and

A. "Slippers?"

B. "What?"

A. "Do you want some slippers?"

  (**B** *looks at his feet, baffled.*)

C. And then, just as he's about to answer her question

A toilet flushes

B. A toilet flushes?

A. A toilet *does* flush

B. But who flushed the toilet?

  (Beat.)

C. A debt collector did.

Scene Seventeen

For the first time, we find ourselves in a real scene with real people. Apart from a few key moments, the storytellers are no longer listening to each other or performing as a unit. Instead, they're in their own worlds and any direct address is between them and the audience.

A.   **B.**   **C.**
An old woman   A young man   A debt collector

B. I'll

A young man stands in a kitchen and sees a man

Sees like

An *old* man

Come in and sit down as if he was expecting him

As if they were both expecting him

What the hell is this?!

C. A debt collector comes back into the kitchen and sees a man

Well, no

Sees a kid in an expensive suit that doesn't even fit him standing there

Dithering

He was gone for two minutes

Who the hell is this?!

A. And then an old woman standing in an apartment in Moscow, Russia realises that she doesn't remember who these two men are or

Why they are here or

Even what they

Wait

Did somebody just say something?

But also realises, remembers

That when there are strangers in your home

Tired, troubled looking men

You ask the question all Russians know isn't really a question

"Tea?"

  (Beat.)

B. A young man wonders whether to mention that he doesn't like tea

He's Russian

He's *still* Russian

He just thinks that this particular situation might not be the best time to *get into tea*

C. A debt collector thinks

God, he'd love a cup of tea

Brewed the Russian way so you're bouncing off the walls

And yes, you could say that it's wrong to take tea from the woman he's about to tell

ENOUGH GAMES, PAY THE FUCK UP!

But then

B. Unable to think of anything to say

Unable to ever think of anything to say

C. Why the hell not?

B. Fuck

Ah

B. Jesus

A. "Well?"

B & C. "Yes"

> (*They look at each other – a macho "I said it first" moment.*)

C. "But Gran, we'll make it"

B. "We will?"

A. And so the two men go to make tea together

Isn't that, in this bandits on the street cats being stolen day and age, something rather special?

"I'll find the good teacups."

> (**B** *and* **C** *make tea while* **A** *shuffles around them, in her own world.*)

B. A young man watches the old guy spoon tea into a teapot

That's enough tea, doesn't he know that that's like ten times more than enough tea?

C. A debt collector halves the amount he would normally brew

Kid doesn't look like he can handle much of anything

And then he says

Quietly

"So

Who are you?"

B. Who is he?

C. Relative would be useful

Someone to take some responsibility around here

B. She came in looking for help and he

Helped her

C. Is he mute or just stupid?

B. But he doesn't know who this guy is, people get the wrong idea and so

C. "Well?"

B. "It's complicated"

C. "Who you are

Is

Complicated?"

B. "We see each other around"

C. "*What?*"

B. "I live in the building"

C. "You live in the building?"

B. "Yeah"

C. "You live in *this* building?"

B. "Has the water boiled?"

C. "No.

(Beat.)

Okay, so you just

Popped by

Tonight

For a cup of tea?"

B. "Oh, no

I'm actually not a big tea drinker"

C. What is wrong with this kid?

B. "I just brought back her cat"

C. Should he get out a medal?

B. "Neighbours need to look out for each other"

C. Oh shut the fuck up

I mean he's right but

Shut the fuck up

B. "It's difficult out there

Scary these days

We all need people we can trust to just

Check in

Ring the bell

Bring back your cat, say

Hey

I haven't heard from you in a few days

How are you / "

C. "Has the water boiled?"

B. "/ doing

No

Yes

I mean

No.

   (An awkward beat.)

What about you?

Also a friendly neighbour?"

C. "Well we'd know each other then

Wouldn't we?"

B. "That is true"

C. "I'm here to help her with her finances"

B. "Oh

Interesting"

C. "Help clear some things up"

B. "Sounds fun"

C. "Maybe you know something about it seeing as you're so involved in her affairs?"

B. "No!

I mean

I'm just"

C. "Yes?"

B. "Has the water boiled?"

C. "Nearly

You were saying?"

B. "I'm just here to bring back her cat!"

(The kettle whistles.)

C. There we go

Helpful neighbours

Not that helpful.

(Beat.)

B.	**C.**
And then a young man watching the water rise in the should have put less tea in it teapot thinks This kid is full of shit	And then a debt collector watching the water rise in the should have put more tea in it teapot thinks

B. This old man's really weird

C. He's not sure whether he's lying or if he just doesn't like him

B. What is this, an FSB interrogation?

C. Why is he sweating?

B. Why does he smell?

C. When will he

B. Who is he

A. "STOPPPPP!

> (**A** *turns her attention back to* **B** *and* **C** *just as boiling water is about to overflow.*)

You need to watch what you're doing or someone is going to get hurt!

Well?

Shall we?"

> (*Beat.*)

B. A young man jumps up as soon as he's sat down, says

"You know what

This has been lovely but

I'm late to a Christmas party

I'm actually late to *my own* Christmas party"

C. "Bullshit"

B. "What?"

A. "Is it Christmas today?"

B. "Yeah, sorry, is the door…"

C. "Where it was ten minutes ago?"

A. "If it's Christmas we should get something special

Some biscuits or

Maybe some jam?"

B. But a young man, free at last from the tea, from the guy, from this good deed turned

Turned he doesn't even know what

Walks back through the hallway, back towards the door

He's never been so pleased to see an unlocked door before

C. And a debt collector, free at last from this kid talking shit, this kid wasting time, who can finally do his job, do the thing you've all been waiting for him to do, turns to the old woman and says

B. Wait

C. What?

B. A young man doesn't leave because the unlocked door is *not* an unlocked door

No, the door is most definitely

"It's locked!"

A. "It's fine, I found biscuits!"

B. "No, you're not

I can't open the door!"

C. Oh

My

God

And so a debt collector stands up

Walks down the hallway

Pushes the kid aside

B. "Ow!"

C. And opens the door.

> *(Beat. No he doesn't.)*

"It's locked"

B. "That's what I just said"

C. "Why is it locked?"

B. "I don't know!"

C. "Well who locked it?!"

A. "I did.

> *(**B** and **C** spin round to find **A** watching them, key around her neck.)*

Bandits on the street, remember?

No

We'll have some tea

We'll have some biscuits

And then we can talk about opening the door"

C. "Right"

B. Really?

Just

C. "Get a move on then"

B. "Right".

> *(Beat. They sit.)*

A. "Well are you going to pour it or not?"

B. "Sorry"

A. "You have to look after us, we're old"

C. "I'm not old"

A. "Look old to me"

C. "Hurry up then!"

B. "I'm doing it"

A. "There we go.

> *(Beat.* **B** *passes them overflowing teacups, hands shaking.* **A** *slurps happily.)*

So"

C. "So"

A. "Tell me about yourselves."

> *(Beat.* **B** *and* **C** *look as if they're never been asked this question before.)*

B. "Oh, er"

C. "We're not just going to sit here and talk about ourselves"

B. "No?"

C. "*No*"

B. "No

This is about

You

Why don't you tell us about

You"

A. "About me?"

C. Christ

B. "How you're doing

How you've been

I mean

B. Merry Christmas"

C. *What* is going on?

B. "How are you?"

> *(Beat. **A** considers – she hasn't been asked this*
> *for as long as she can remember.)*

A. So then an old woman starts to talk

C. Then an old woman starts to really fucking talk

A. She didn't think this morning she'd be talking

That she'd have guests round for tea

That she was going to open the doors to anyone ever again

Couldn't have, not possible, absolutely not! Not after the year that she's

"Wait, what year is it now?"

C. "2019"

A. "No one ever tells you anything anymore, like, maybe she'd like to know"

B. "What?"

A. "Biscuit?"

C. "Sure"

> *(**B** and **C** both take a biscuit.)*

A. And so she starts at the beginning

With the phone calls.

> *(Beat.)*

C. A debt collector listens to an old woman talk about

A. "The phone calls"

C. And he wants to grab her and shout

That's not the beginning you idiot

Things in Russia don't just happen for

A. "No reason

Nothing"

C. There's always a story before the phone calls

A meeting with someone sitting pretty in their office

Looking friendly

Wearing a

(**C** *looks at* **B** *but brushes the thought away.*)

Suit

And he didn't call

A. "Every minute of every hour"

C. It must've been another agency who rang her

People who get out loans don't just get out the one

But

Instead

He just eats another

A. "Biscuit?"

B. "Thanks"

C. And stares at the kid

B. Why does the old guy keep staring?

C. Finish your tea and fuck off.

(*Beat.*)

B. A young man listens to an old woman talk about

A. "The phone calls"

B. And he wants to stand up and say

Wants to stand up and shout

Just turn off your phone Gran

Just block the bloody number

It's 2019

Don't you know that it's 2019 and he has his own party to get to?!

But instead he just eats another

A. "Biscuit?"

B. And tries to finish his tea

C. "Pour me another"

B. But it's hard, okay, if your nervous system isn't used to caffeine

And it's hard, okay, when there's a psychopath staring you down

What is this?

C. Does anyone know who this is?

(Beat.)

A. "And then he took Sally"

C. "Who did?"

A. "*He* did"

C. "*You* did?"

B. "I don't know who Sally is!"

C. "You don't know who Sally is?"

A. "She's my cat!"

B. "Right

Okay

She's your cat"

C. He doesn't know who Sally is?

A. "It's a classic

A scare tactic

How else does a cat get out of an apartment like this?"

B. "Fall out the window?"

A. "She'd locked all the windows"

B. "Run out the door?"

A. "She'd locked both the doors"

B. "Expect the unexpected

Moscow /"

C. "Is he your neighbour, Gran?"

B. "Russia"

(Beat.)

A. "Is who my neighbour Gran?"

C. "Him"

B. "Me?"

A. "No"

C. BINGO!

Because a debt collector might be old, might be getting kind of old, but he knows, like all debt collectors across Moscow, Russia know

When someone is lying

And he also knows

C. That it's the ones with the baby faces in the expensive suits that you need to watch out for.

    (*Beat.* **C** *sits back satisfied, before...*)

So wait

Who the fuck is he then?

A. "BANG!"

    (**B** *and* **C** *both jump.*)

C. "What?"

A. "An explosion!"

B. "Where?"

A. "In the courtyard

Gold!"

C. "Gold explosions don't happen in courtyards"

A. "And meatballs"

B. "And

Sorry

And meatballs?"

A. "Couldn't even make meatballs because of the noise"

B. "Of the explosion?"

A. "Of the ringing"

B. "But who set off the explosion?"

C. "No one!"

A. "The man who kept ringing"

B. "But why was he ringing?"

A. "Who kept leaving the notes"

C. "Did you ever read what they said?"

A. "And all because"

B. What the hell's going on

A. "All because"

C. Who the hell is this kid

A. "All because he said

You owe money"

B. "Sorry

What?"

A. "You owe money and you need to pay it back or bad things are going to happen"

B. "Fuck"

A. "I know!

Fuck

I've never owed money

Not to anyone

Not ever

And even if I did

Even if somehow I did

Is it enough to warrant that kind of harassment?

Until you can't sleep

Can't eat

Go out

Make meatballs

Until you're so busy pretending you're not there, that one day you realise it's true

You don't exist anymore!"

B. ENOUGH!

A young man stands up in a kitchen in Moscow, Russia and looks at an

Old woman

And looks at an old man

And then he looks at

Sally's not even here, fuck you Sally!

And he knows in that moment that he has to get out

His Christmas party is starting

His Christmas party is literally starting and his

You were all there with him and she needed money, she asked him for money and

And

A. "Why are you standing up?"

C. "I'd also like to know why you're standing up"

B. And so a young man takes an old woman's hand again, looks her straight in the eyes again, and does the thing he does everyday, the thing he's so good at and says

"Gran, I need you to do something for me

Do you understand what I'm saying?"

A. And as an old woman feels those sweaty, small hands again, smells that strong, bitter perfume again, looks into those dark, *his* dark eyes again, she

Remembers

"You're the boy from the bank!

Why are you holding my hand?"

> *(Beat. **B** tries to keep it together but he is suddenly very aware of **C** watching him.)*

B. "I need you to unlock the doors

I need to leave now"

A. "Okay, it's okay

No reason to get upset

I'll go and unlock the doors

Just give me a minute."

(Beat. **A** *winks, then exits.)*

C. "One of the boys from the bank

That makes a lot more sense"

B. "Erm"

C. "I always wondered what you kids looked like

And you know, you're

Exactly

What I imagined"

B. "I don't know what that means"

C. "But what I can't figure out is

What's the cat got to do with it?

Did you feel guilty or something?"

B. "What?

No

Of course not"

C. "Of course not"

B. "I don't understand

What is this?"

C. "Oh give it up

Stop pretending for one minute!"

B. "I /"

C. "Fuck off so I can clean up your mess."

> *(**A** re-appears.)*

A. "Ready!

> *(Beat.)*

Who was leaving again?"

C. "He was"

A. And so an old woman shows the boy back down the hallway

B. "Wait"

A. Back through the door

B. "I mean"

A. Back onto the landing

B. "I don't"

A. Hands him for a biscuit for the road and says

"Thank you

You were very helpful".

> *(Beat.)*

C. A debt collector doesn't know who the kid from the bank was or why he was here

But he can't be too high up in the food chain if he all he did was sweat and *not* drink tea

And so he turns to the old woman who's just come back inside and says

"Sit down

We need to talk"

B. A young man stands on a landing in Moscow, Russia and he feels

Better

Yeah

He feels better

Let's just get to the party!

> *(Beat.* **B** *looks at the audience indignantly. Is this how they see him – as the bad guy?)*

Wait but

What did he say?

C. "Do you remember what we were talking about before he arrived?"

B. Yeah he works at the bank

Okay and so what?

C. "The phone calls

Day in and day out?"

B. Exactly what he imagined?

C. "The explosion?"

B. Yeah he's a bank manager

And yeah he does look exactly like a bank manager

C. "The notes?"

B. But if there's a mess, it's not his

C. "Because you *do* owe money"

B. I mean he brought back her cat

C. "And you *do* need to pay it back"

B. On the day of his party

C. "And that's why I'm here"

B. He's

C. "Ivan"

B. Guilty?

C. "Well?"

B. Guilty?!

A. Except that at that precise moment, as the old woman looks into the *debt collector's* eyes

Feels the tight

C. Loose

A. *Tight* grip of his hand around her wrist

B. The bell rings!

C. The bell doesn't ring

A. No the bell *does* ring

And an old woman forgets all about what the nice man in the jacket was saying

C. You've got to be kidding me

A. Runs down the hall, unlocks the door and sees

B. The bank manager!

Thought he was gone?

Thought his story was over?

No

He's not going to run away with his tail between his legs because some creep in a jacket is

Misinformed

He's ending this on his own terms

And so he walks, no, strides, back through the doors, back through the hallway, back into the kitchen, and gives the old man, now cowering in his chair, a

Good

Hard

Er

Look.

> *(Beat.* **A**, **B** *and* **C** *find themselves back where they started.)*

C. A debt collector has been in plenty of

Situations

Before

But this one is really taking the piss

I mean doesn't the kid know that when a debt collector tells you to get lost, you get lost?

A. And then an old woman

Surprised by how many guests she's had today

Years of nothing and then this

Asks the question all Russians know isn't really a question

"Tea?"

B. "*Tea?*"

C. "Yes, tea would be great

In fact

> *(***C*** *stands in front of the used teacups.)*

You were going to get some nice teacups"

A. "I was?"

C. "You were

From the bedroom"

A. "The bedroom?"

C. "Why not?"

A. "Well, yes

That makes sense

Tea in nice teacups".

(**A** *exits.*)

C. "What do you think you're doing?"

B. "Er"

C. "Er er er –

Shut up

Did the bank send you?

Is this another initiative and

Wait

Are you the guinea pig?"

B. "No!"

C. "So you don't work for the bank?"

B. "No

Yes

I do

I *am* a bank manager

I'm actually a branch manager"

C. "I don't care what they scribble on your badge"

B. "And I don't like your tone"

C. "Excuse me?"

B. "I think there's been a misunderstanding"

C. "Was that when you started talking about my tone?"

B. "Maybe"

C. "We're not in your office

I'm not one of your pensioners"

B. "And this isn't my mess

She asked for money

She asked, voluntarily for money

And I helped her when no one else would.

(Beat.)

The person you should be directing this

Toxic"

C. "*Toxic*"

B. "Energy towards

Is the guy who's been driving her crazy

I mean didn't you hear her

The phone calls

The explosions

Stealing Sally

Who is this bastard?

*(**C** laughs.)*

Why are you laughing?"

C. And then a debt collector realises that this kid is even stupider than he looks

What does he think happens six months down the line?

"Nice to meet you then"

B. "What?"

*(**A** re-enters.)*

C. "Guess that makes me the bastard"

A. "Why did you tell me the teacups were in the bedroom when they're right here on the table?

> *(Beat.)*

Coo-coo!

Is someone making tea?"

C. "I think we're going to need something stronger

Do you have any cognac?"

A. "Cognac, no

Vodka

Yes"

C. "Perfect"

A. "But I'll have to go find it"

C. "Please".

> *(**A** exits.)*

You see a debt collector's realised what he should have realised a long time ago

No one's going to do the right thing here

No one's going to hand him what's his here

No

He's just going to have to solve it himself

Like he always does

And so

B. A young man watches a debt collector

Of course he's a debt collector

C. He starts sorting through the kitchen

B. Ransacking the kitchen

C. Methodically

B. Violently

B. "Hey!"

C. "Hey!"

B. "Hey

What, no"

> (**A** *re-enters.*)

A. "Did we say vodka or cognac?"

C. "Cognac"

> (**A** *exits.*)

B. "What are you doing?"

C. "What does it look like I'm doing?"

B. "You can't just take an old woman's stuff!"

C. "We're doing the same thing

We're just doing it differently"

> (**A** *re-enters.*)

B. "I'm calling the police"

A. "No cognac, just my homemade 33 Siberian herb liqueur

Who's calling the police?"

C. "He is

And he's going to call them and explain it

But this time from the *beginning* beginning"

A. "The *beginning* beginning..."

*(**A** notices **C** rifling through cupboards.)*

A. Excuse me, what are you doing?"

C. "I'm searching for teacups"

A. "But we're having my herb liqueur, remember?"

B. "They'll help!"

A. "Who will help?"

B. "The police!"

*(**A** and **C** laugh.)*

C. "You've been watching too many American films

Nothing that I'm doing is illegal here"

A. "Why would what you're doing be illegal?"

B. "Because it's him!"

A. "Who?"

B. *"Him!*

The /"

A. "Let's just all calm down for a minute

Everyone is talking so fast

I'm going to get us some glasses"

B. "No"

A. "No to my liqueur?!"

B. "No to any more beverages!"

A. "What have you got against my liqueur?"

B. *"Listen"*

A. "Found them!"

B. "Gran!"

(**B** *snatches the bottle from* **A**.)

A. "Are you pouring?"

B. "I'm fine"

A. "You don't seem fine"

C. "He'll be fine when he's drunk"

B. "I'm not drinking"

C. "Don't be rude"

A. "Now listen

This is an old recipe passed down generation to generation

It will make *everything* better

To making everything better!

(**A** *pours, they drink.* **B** *retches, even* **C** *pulls a face.*)

Energising, isn't it?"

C. "What's in this?!"

A. "I told you

33 herbs"

C. "And when did you make it?"

A. "Before my third husband died

Another?"

B. "We need to call the police"

C. "We need to have another shot of whatever that is"

B. "They can fix this!"

A. "Oh come off it

They can't and they won't

A. The only difference between that man and the police is that the police are allowed to carry guns

And they have nice fur hats

To the hats!

> *(They drink.)*

It grows on you, doesn't it?"

B. "Let's just go for a walk"

A. "I'm not going for a walk on

What day is it again?"

C. "Christmas Eve"

A. "To Christmas Eve!"

> *(They drink.)*

B. "But you're not safe"

A. "Well of course I'm not safe!

In Moscow?

In Russia?

To Russia!

> *(They drink.)*

But

If I'm going to be stabbed by some bandit, better in the comfort of my own home"

B. "But the money"

A. "Oh don't worry, I've hidden it extremely well"

C. "To hiding it well!"

> *(They drink.)*

So where did you hide it?"

(*A looks at* **C** *– does she see him for what he really is?*)

A. "You'll need to get me a lot drunker for that"

C. "Well then to getting a lot drunker for that"

B. "I can't drink anymore"

C. "Oh but we can

Again

> (*They drink.*)

And again"

> (*They drink.*)

A. "I need to sit down"

> (*A sits down – apparently out of it.* **C** *resumes his search.*)

B. "You can't just keep doing this

She thinks you're her guest!"

C. "And whose fault is that?"

B. "She's confused!"

> (*A looks up – more lucid than expected.*)

C. "Just

Listen

You're the bad guy either way

You can be the bad guy who leaves and pretends it's not happening

Or you can be the bad guy who stays and gets the job done

Which is it?"

B. And so a bank manager

C. And a debt collector

B. Search an old woman's apartment for money

C. Finally

A. While an old woman watches them

B. "How do you even know you'll find money?"

C. "I know, I know"

A. "What were you looking for again?"

C. "Biscuits"

> (**A** *looks at the biscuits on the table.*)

A. "Are you sure it was biscuits?"

C. "Maybe vodka"

> (**A** *looks at the vodka on the table.*)

B. "How can you be sure?"

A. "Are you sure?"

C. "Yes

YES

People always say there's isn't money

But when you look a little harder

There it is"

A. "Biscuits *and* vodka?"

C. "Can you tell her to shut up?"

B. "But what if you don't?"

A. "Or vodka and biscuits?"

C. "That's not an option"

B. "What does that mean?"

A. "I don't believe you"

C. "It means I make them give it to me"

B. "And what does *that* mean?"

A. "I don't believe you!!"

C. "WILL YOU JUST SHUT UP!"

     (*B and* **C** *spin round to find* **A**, *standing, holding the small sharp knife from earlier.*)

B. "Why have you got a knife?

   Why has she got a knife?"

C. "I don't know"

B. "Did *you* bring that?"

C. "No"

A. "It's mine"

C. "See"

B. "Okay

     (Beat.)

  So"

C. "Why are you holding it?"

A. "Haven't you been listening to anything I've been saying?

  Bandits on the streets

  Bandits in the home"

C. "Enough games

  Let's just

  Give me the knife"

A. "Why would I give you the knife?"

C. "Because you're drunk"

A. "No I'm not"

C. "You just did six shots"

A. "Seven

Just like you

And I've been drinking that stuff for decades"

C. "You're going to hurt yourself

Give it to me

Now"

A. "I've got no intention of hurting myself and you haven't answered my question"

C. "What question?"

A. "What it is that you're looking for"

C. "I told you already"

A. "Vodka?

> (**A** *throws the vodka bottle at him.*)

Biscuits?

> (**A** *throws the biscuits at him.*)

What's next?

Jam?"

C. "Now don't get all crazy

I've tried to explain"

A. "You haven't explained

You've just made a mess"

B. "It's him, Gran"

C. "I'm taking back what you owe"

A. "Bullshit"

C. "I tried to tell you"

A. "Bullshit"

B. "From the /"

*(**A** suddenly turns to **B**.)*

A. "And who are you?"

B. "Gran"

A. "Don't call me Gran"

B. "Okay

It's me

I brought back Sally, remember?"

A. "Sally's in the bedroom"

B. "No but she went missing

Earlier?"

A. "How does a cat escape an apartment like this?"

B. "He took her!"

C. "I didn't take her!"

A. "Now get out

Before I run this knife through the both of you"

B. "Yes

Okay

That's what we want too

I have a Christmas party to get to"

A. "You're lying

It's not Christmas"

C. "It's Christmas and you're confused"

A. "I'm not confused!"

B. "Just give us the keys"

A. "Why would I give you the keys?"

B. "Because you locked all the doors, remember?"

A. "Don't ask me if I remember

I remember, I remember, I remember, I remember

And I'm *not* giving you the keys"

B. "Okay

Then why don't *you* unlock the doors?

Tell us when you've done it

And then we'll leave, okay?

*(A long pause. Finally, **A** nods.)*

Okay."

C. "No"

B. "*What*?!"

C. "I'm not leaving without my money"

B. "She has a knife"

C. "Do you think I've never dealt with a knife before?"

A. "Do you think I've never dealt with a man inside my apartment before?"

B. "Gran, it's him, he wants your money

I'm just trying to get to my party"

A. "I'm not doing anything until you both leave my apartment"

C. "And I'm not doing anything until you give me my money"

B. "The keys around your neck

I'm just going to"

(*Beat.*)

And then a young man steps forward to show her that he doesn't mean any harm

He never meant any harm

He just wants to go home

C. And then a debt collector sees the kid lurch forward suddenly

As if he's never been around someone holding a knife before

Someone really scared before

A. And then an old woman sees the boy with a baby face

A face you don't see so much anymore

Reach towards her as if to grab her, strangle her, do something bad to her

And she realises he was out to get her

He was out to get *her* this whole time

Of course

(*Beat.*)

A & C. And so she does what all scared people do in situations like this

B. She hands him the keys!

C. No

B. She throws him the keys?

A. No

B. She bends down, slides the keys across the floor like they do in the movies and

B. Ow

She stabs him!

C. And he falls back into the table

B. Sorry

C. Back into the chairs

A. Sorry

C. Back into the cat food dispenser, sugar pot, framed photo of a man in military uniform

B. Oh God

I'm so sorry

C. And as each item falls and breaks one by one

Money

Lots and lots of money.

Scene Eighteen

Signoff.

C. A debt collector leaves an apartment.

> *(Beat. A moment where anything could happen – remorse, a confession.* **C** *considers it, until he doesn't.)*

Wait, were you expecting more?

A debt collector is pinned down by a heroic bank manager until the police arrive to take him away in handcuffs!

A debt collector pays off an old woman's debt himself and they meet every Sunday to share stories of the good old days!

A debt collector looks at the bloodstained money and realises that debt collecting is bad?

No

This is a Russian story

And that's not how our stories end.

> *(Beat.)*

Did he take the money?

Of course he did

You can wash blood out of banknotes

Her loan is settled and the phone calls

Although there weren't nearly as many as she seemed to think

Will stop.

> *(Beat.)*

C. You see, Russia isn't one of those countries that holds you by the hand

It throws you in the deep end like a father teaching his son how to swim

Says

Go on, show me what you've got, fight for yourself because no one else will

And that's what he does, for himself, for his family

The rest doesn't concern him

Debt is debt is debt is debt

And Russia is the same as it has always been

Bitter, but beautiful.

> *(Beat.)*

And so a debt collector

Now at the front door of her apartment block by the way

Picks up a magazine to cover his head

And hurries home in the rain

Olga's making vinegret tonight.

> *(Beat.)*

B. A young man leaves an apartment

Waits for the lights to turn from red to green

Crosses the road, and takes the Metro home to his Christmas Eve party.

> *(Beat.)*

I know what you're thinking

But what about the stab wound?

What about the incredibly dramatic stabbing we all

Just

Witnessed?

> *(Beat.)*

But no

Thanks but

He's okay

Didn't go very deep, no internal damage and he's young

Isn't the whole point that he's young?

No

The worst part, really, is that he's ruined a bloody expensive suit!

And the best part?

There is something quite cool about turning up to your own party

With a stab wound.

> *(Beat. **B** falters slightly.)*

The blue line's closed so he changes at Arbatskaya and walks down Tverskaya

"Moscow's Oxford Street"

In the pouring rain

You hear about the snow here but you don't really hear about the rain

The freezing rain.

> *(Beat. He's not sure how to put a positive spin on this.)*

He passes couples in coffee houses

B. Do you know how much Russians love coffee houses?

Americano? More like Russiano!

Women waiting for their drivers to carry them home

And men eating sushi

On Christmas Eve!

> *(He wobbles,)*

It is so beautiful and it is so

Gold

How did it get so gold?

> *(Beat.* **B** *sits down, exhausted.)*

But although the gold spills out onto the street, bouncing off puddles and tinted car windows and illuminating him, too, all in gold

A young man suddenly feels farther away from it all than he ever has

Knows now

Finally

That he's just a boy from a South Eastern district of Moscow with rain filling his shoes.

> *(Beat.* **B** *looks at the audience, finally seeing himself as they see him.)*

Did you all know this whole time?

> *(Beat.)*

A. An old woman stands in a kitchen in Moscow, Russia and clears away teacups

One

Two

Four five did she have *this* many guests?

Must have been quite the party

Vodka and mayonnaise, a half eaten biscuit

> (**A** *finishes the biscuit.*)

A banknote?

Someone must have dropped that

And a knife

> (**A** *wipes it on her cardigan.*)

Need to be careful with that

Where did all this clutter come from?

And who broke the teacup!

> (*Beat.*)

But despite all the mess

Despite not knowing when they arrived or what their names even were

Why they got so excited

Why they left so abruptly

Despite all of that

She had a nice day, no, she had the *best* day she'd had in years

She can't wait to call her daughter and tell her about it!

I mean, who cares about one broken teacup?

"In each chipped cup, there's a story

Some time spent with friends"

Whether you remember them or not.

> (*Beat.*)

A. And so as she hums along to the rain with Sally purring at her feet, she looks out at the city

Her city

And smiles at the glow of the buildings across the road and the

Wait

When did that get put up?

> (**A** *is transfixed as the storytellers come back into her story – but not* **B**. *He's done, for now, and just watches from the sidelines.*)

C. "We're not as different as we think

We're stronger, united"

A. With a picture of a man, holding out money and smiling

And so an old woman thinks

Well of course and why not!?

If there's anything today has taught her it's that together, we *are* better

She'll visit tomorrow.

> (*The storytellers share a look that says – is that it? Are we done? They nod. Blackout.*)

The End

9 780573 000423